THE
DOLLS' CLOTHES
COLLECTION

CHRISTINA HARRIS

David & Charles

A DAVID & CHARLES BOOK

First published in the UK in 2003

Distributed in North America
by F&W Publications, Inc.
4700 East Galbraith Road
Cincinnati, OH 45236
1-800-289-0963

A catalogue record for this book is available from the British Library.

ISBN 0 7153 1468 8 hardback
ISBN 0 7153 1469 6 paperback (USA only)

Printed in Hong Kong by Dai Nippon Printing for David & Charles
Brunel House   Newton Abbot   Devon

Executive Editor: Cheryl Brown
Desk Editor: Sandra Pruski
Executive Art Editor: Ali Myer
Senior Designer: Prudence Rogers
Production Controller: Ros Napper

Visit our website at www.davidandcharles.co.uk

David & Charles books are available from all good bookshops;
alternatively you can contact our Orderline on (0)1626 334555 or write to
us at FREEPOST EX2110, David & Charles Direct, Newton Abbot,
TQ12 4ZZ (no stamp required UK mainland).

Contents

olls are an important part of our heritage and women and girls of all ages love collecting and dressing them. Making an outfit for a doll can be a rewarding challenge both for the doll artist, for whom the costume is an essential part of the doll, and for the collector to know she is able to make beautiful outfits in which to display her dolls.

I have created fifteen outfits from the late 1800s through to the 1950s, which are diverse in style and varied within the wardrobe of each period. The designs do not represent authentic antique costumes, rather they give the impression of the period of the time. There are patterns for underclothing compatible with the outfits, as well as hats, boots and shoes to complete the look.

The clothes are made mainly on a sewing machine with hems and finishing work done by hand though it is possible to do everything by hand if you prefer. Most of the designs are simple enough for the novice seamstress to construct, though a few will need some degree of experience. With patience you should be able to achieve good results. Read the *'Before you Begin'* section and all the instructions right through before cutting or sewing.

Choosing an outfit

Selecting the appropriate costume for your doll depends on the doll that you are dressing as faces and proportions can vary greatly. A young girl doll's proportions can be much chubbier than a lady doll making a lady's costume quite unsuitable. An antique doll dressed in one of the 1950s costumes will not look right, nor would a Shirley Temple doll dressed in the Egyptian chemise. Use your judgement when deciding on your costume and do use a doll stand. It gives support when dressing and will display the doll to its best advantage when the costume is completed. Choose a stand that fits snugly around the doll's waist with a base that stands securely. It should go over the underwear and under the petticoat and outer clothing.

Measuring for a good fit

The basic patterns fit dolls: 35.5-40.5cm (14-16in), 43-48cm (17-19in), 51-56cm (20-22in) and 58-63.5cm (23-25in).
There is no such thing as an average doll. They are all unique and can vary dramatically in their basic body measurements. It is important that you take your doll's measurements, compare them to the pattern and make any necessary adjustments before cutting out. Measurements of the doll used in each of the patterns are given. The seam allowance is already in the pattern for those measurements, but if your doll's measurements differ, remember to add a 6mm (¼in) seam allowance to the pattern.

The basic measurements are:
1 Chest width from under arms across chest.
2 Back width from under arms across back.
3 Waist circumference.
4 Waist length from cervical point at base of neck to natural waistline.
5 Hips circumference at widest point.
6 Shoulder width from neck to arm joint.
7 Sleeve length from arm joint at top of shoulder to wrist (or wherever you want the sleeve to end). Arm should be down.
8 Wrist circumference. If the fingers are spread, make allowances so that the sleeve will go over the hand.
9 Leg length from waist to hemline and from crotch to hemline.
10 Head circumference.

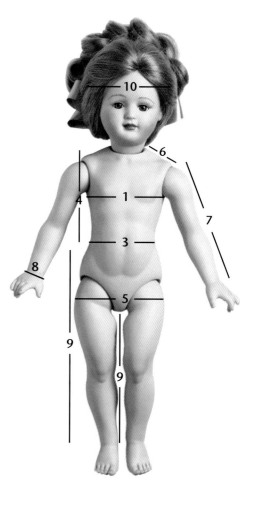

Trace the pattern pieces and adjust them according to your doll's measurements. Then trace the adjusted patterns on to lightweight card, transferring all the markings, and cut out. Lay the card pattern piece on the wrong side of the fabric and draw around it with a ballpoint pen.

Try the garment on the doll several times during sewing. A 6mm (¼in) error can make a big difference when working on a small scale.

To make a shoe that fits your doll's foot, match the foot to the sole pattern. Small adjustments can be made if the difference is not too great. To make your own pattern place your doll's foot on a piece of paper and carefully draw around the foot, holding the pencil at right angles to the foot. This gives an accurate template.

Adapting patterns

To ensure a good fit when adjusting patterns to fit a larger doll, take your doll's basic measurements and, using tissue paper, add the measurements to the original pattern pieces by cutting where indicated inserting tissue paper taped in place and redrawing the outline. When you have adjusted all the pattern pieces use them to cut out a mock-up garment from cotton fabric, (curtain lining fabric works well and is inexpensive). Baste it together, don't use pins as they can stick to a cloth body and may scratch porcelain or composition bodies. Then try it on your doll, inside out and make any other adjustments before you cut the pattern out for real.

When adjusting patterns to fit a smaller doll, use the guidelines as before but this time overlap the pieces before redrawing the outline. The diagrams below show basic adjustments to the main pattern pieces and where you should alter them. The patterns can be made larger by cutting where shown, inserting and taping in place tissue paper, shown as shaded areas in the diagrams. The patterns can be made smaller by cutting where shown and overlapping the pattern pieces.

To eliminate bust darts for dolls with flat chests, pin the dart in the paper pattern, lay the pattern on the fabric and cut out. Don't worry about the excess pattern paper in the dart area as long as the fabric is smooth underneath.

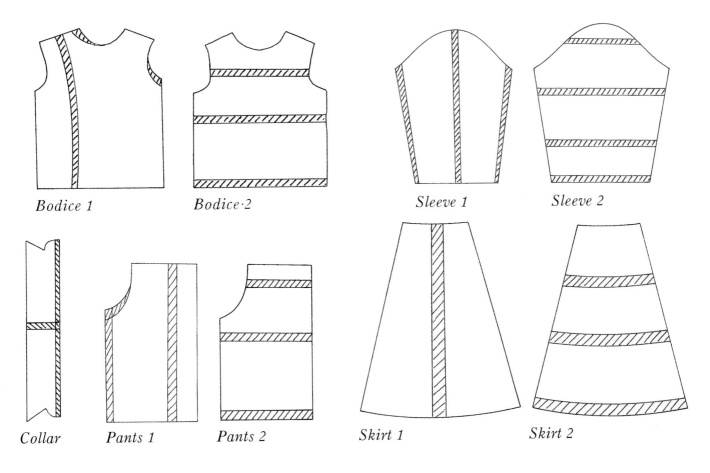

Bodice 1   *Bodice·2*   *Sleeve 1*   *Sleeve 2*

Collar   *Pants 1*   *Pants 2*   *Skirt 1*   *Skirt 2*

Tools and equipment

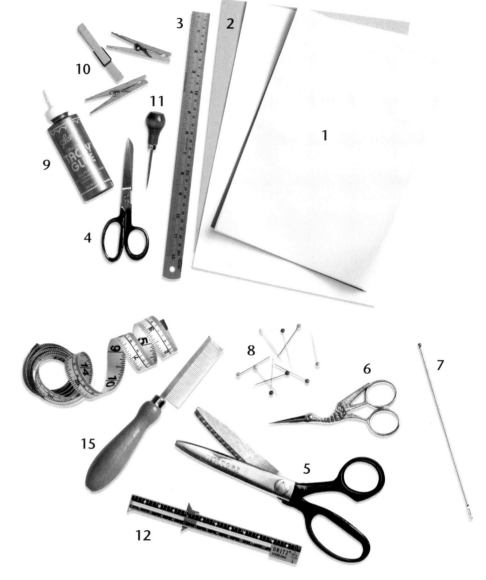

Along with basic sewing items such as pins, needles, tape measure, fabric shears and a sewing machine, a list of useful items for making up the outfits, including shoes and hats, includes:

1 Tracing and tissue paper
2 Lightweight cardboard for shoe soles
3 Straight edge ruler
4 Scissors for cutting card
5 Pinking shears (if your machine does not have a zigzag stitch)
6 Small sharp scissors
7 Bodkin or safety pin for threading elastic through casings
8 Glass-headed pins
9 Fabric glue
10 Clothes pegs for holding shoe and sole together while gluing
11 Awl for punching tiny holes
12 Gauge ruler to measure button placements and hems
13 Sleeve board for pressing tiny sleeves
14 Travel iron to reach small places
15 Cat comb for fur fabrics

Choosing fabrics

The fabric amounts given for the costumes are on the generous side. In many cases such as skirts you will need the length of the fabric called for but may have fabric width left over. This is because the patterns must be laid out in the direction of the arrows. Fabric amounts for the smaller items are not given, as scraps of material would be sufficient. Use your own judgement on trims and laces.

The fabrics that you choose, whether they are modern, vintage, or possibly from old clothes, should represent the era as closely as possible. Man-made fibres such as nylon were not widely used until the 1950s so would not be appropriate for costumes before that time. Natural fabrics gather and hang better than man-made fibres and 100 per cent cotton will hold a pleat or crease more successfully than cotton mixed with polyester. Lawn, batiste, calico, poplin, dotted Swiss voile, broderie anglaise, organza, silk, and satin all make up well and add to the feel of the clothes. Woollens should be lightweight, the heavier wools are bulky and may prove too thick when turning collars, cuffs and corners. Consider velveteen as an alternative to velvet for smaller dolls, as it is lighter in weight. Velvet, which is heavier, should only be used on larger dolls.

Colour is very important when making up period costumes. Bright primary colours were not used much before the 1950s and turquoise, lime green and orange were unheard of. A costume from the Victorian or Edwardian period should reflect the colours of a conventional and conservative era. Deep violet, burgundy, rose, smoky greys and blues, olive and hunter green, black, brown and camel were widely in use. White was a colour of purity and innocence and was frequently used for Sunday best and for babies and young children, often with decorative ribbons and embroidery in pastel shades of pink, blue and primrose yellow. You can be a little freer with costumes from the 1920s onward, introducing primary colours for a more adventurous feel. The colour of the doll's hair, eyes and

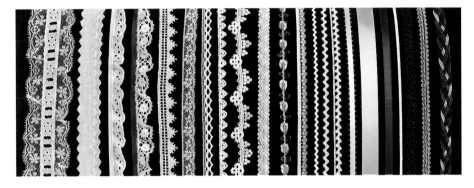

skin tone should also be considered when selecting your fabric.

The scale of the print in a fabric is important when choosing fabrics. Scale down the sizes when you choose buttons and trims as well. Search your drawers and boxes for forgotten items such as trims, beads and jewellery that might be appropriate to the period.

Choosing trimmings

Flea markets and antique shops are a good source and it doesn't matter if they look a bit dingy, as long as they are sound and not too badly stained. You can safely launder them by hand, adding a small amount of non-chlorine bleach to the wash. Don't use lace that contains nylon on vintage costumes, it looks too new. Use cotton lace or, better still, old lace, which is far more delicate and detailed in comparison.

Lace plays an important role when creating an antique look on period dolls. It can be used in many ways to create different images. Use it around necklines, collars and cuffs, to define a pintucked yoke, to decorate a bodice or finish off a hemline. A bit of lace transforms the plainest garment and is almost a must on underwear, bonnets and parasols. Flat or gathered lace can be stitched to the

surface of the fabric or set underneath a hemline or cuff so only the edge is visible. It can be enclosed between fabric and lining for a neat finish and delicate flat lace can be whipstitched to the edge of the fabric.

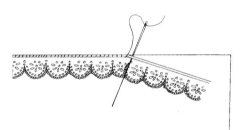

Working with fur fabrics

Imitation man-made fur fabrics have a woven or knitted backing. Woven backings are far superior and give a richer and more realistic look to the garment, as the pile is denser. Mohair plush comes from the alpaca goat and is quite expensive but it is not necessary to use it as long as a quality imitation fur can be obtained. Do not buy fur fabric if you can see the backing through the fur when you curl it backwards.

Imitation fur fabric comes in a variety of colours, animal prints and pile length. Take the length of the pile into consideration with the size of the

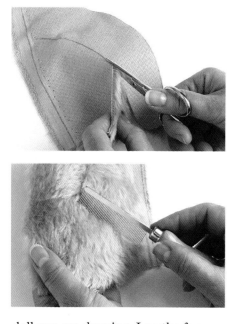

Helpful sewing hints

- For machine sewing a size 10 (70) or 11 (75) needle is good for cotton and silks and size14 (90) for heavier fabrics like woollens and velvet. A ballpoint needle prevents snagging when sewing silk. Use a small stitch when sewing dolls clothes. Change the needle when it becomes blunt and keep your machine well oiled and free from lint.
- When stitching material such as velvet or satin, sew slowly pulling gently on the fabric and place your pins at right angles to the stitching line to prevent the material from walking.
- If you are using a fabric that frays easily, finish raw edges that will remain raw by machine zigzag stitch, cutting with pinking shears or overcasting by hand before stitching together.
- Tissue paper placed under leather or fur fabric when sewing will help the fabric run smoothly on the machine.
- Always cut ribbon on the bias. A tiny amount of fabric glue or Fray Check will stop it from fraying.
- It is not necessary to wash cotton fabrics before use but they should always be pressed before cutting out.
- For hand sewing a thin needle like a milliner or darner is easier to use than an ordinary sharp. They are longer and thinner and once you get used to them you will probably find a shorter needle quite awkward.
- Thread the needle as it comes off the spool, knotting the end you cut off. This will prevent the thread snarling.
- Thread is expensive so if you have a lot of ruffles or gathering stitches to do, use a lesser quality thread as it will be removed anyway. If you use quality thread for gathers, when it is pulled out save it for hand stitching.
- When hemming or blind stitching use a single thread and close, neat stitches. Cotton or cotton polyester mixed thread should match the garment colour as closely as possible. Use silk thread on silk fabrics – strands pulled from the fabric and used as thread make stitches nearly invisible.
- Dressmakers' pins are best for lightweight fabrics. They are a bit longer and thinner than ordinary pins, which makes working on heavier fabrics easier. Use silk pins on silk and taffeta. Pins can become blunt so if they catch the fabric replace them.
- Use a piece of muslin or an old tea towel as a pressing cloth to prevent damage when working with delicate or antique fabrics. When ironing woollens the pressing cloth should be slightly damp and the fabric ironed slowly so that the dampness is driven into the fabric below.
- When pressing velvet, lay the fabric face down on to a Turkish towel to prevent crushing the pile, then gently steam press on the wrong side of the fabric.

doll you are dressing. Lay the fur fabric with the pile facing downwards and place the pattern pieces with the arrow pointing in the direction of the pile. Draw around the patterns with a ballpoint pen. When cutting out make small snips using just the points of your scissors. Cut only the fabric backing, not the pile. Linings should be cut slightly smaller so that when they are stitched together, the fur will curl under slightly to hide the lining. Always use glass-headed pins with fur fabric. Trim the fur back 6mm (¼in) around each piece and pin at right angles to the stitching line, pushing the fur down into the piece as you pin. Try not to trap fur outside the stitching line, but if you do, use a cat comb to tease it out. Use a number 14 (90) or 16 (100) needle in your machine and if you are working with a knitted backing use a ballpoint needle. If you need to press the lining, hold the iron just above the lining side and force steam into the fabric. Press the seams with your fingers while the fabric is still warm. Never iron the fur.

Basic Sewing Techniques & Stitches

*T*he following sewing techniques and basic stitches are referred to in the patterns and used to make the clothes and accessories. Read through the section before starting on a pattern.

Perfect gathers

Using the longest stitch on your machine, run two parallel rows of stitching about 6mm (¼in) apart. Wrap the two top ends round your finger and pull up, distributing the gathers evenly. With right sides together and the gathering stitches facing you, pin at right angles to the straight edge they are being joined to and adjust the gathers. Wind the ends of the threads over the end pins to secure and stitch between the two rows. Fig 1. Pull out the lower row of gathering stitches.

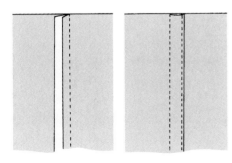

Fig 1

Run and fell seam

This seam is used for strength or to neaten fine fabrics that fray easily. With wrong sides together, run a 6mm (¼in) seam. Trim one of the seam allowances to 3mm (⅛in). Fig 2.

Turn the untrimmed seam allowance over, encasing the trimmed edge, and stitch in place. Fig 3.

Elastic

Shirring elastic is used at the arms, wrists and legs. Wrap the elastic snugly but not tightly round the part of the doll. Mark the elastic and cut it 5cm (2in) from the mark. This gives enough length to pull the elastic up to the mark and secure it. Lightly draw a pencil line on the wrong side of the fabric where the elastic is to go. Secure the end of the elastic at the start of the line and, using a zigzag stitch, pull up the elastic, encasing it in the zigzags as you sew. When you reach the end, secure the elastic at the mark and cut off the extra. If you do not have a zigzag stitch, use a doubled thread to make a casing by hand and weave the elastic through. Fig 4.

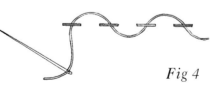

Fig 4

Flat elastic is used for stretch waistbands. Use 6-12mm (¼-½in) elastic. Turn down 6mm (¼in) at the top of the waistline and press. Then turn down a further amount wide enough so the elastic will slip easily through and stitch in place leaving a small gap at the back seam to insert the elastic. Cut a length of elastic 12mm (½in) smaller than the doll's waist measurement and using a safety-pin or bodkin attached to one end, guide it through the casing. When the end of the elastic is about to disappear, secure it with a pin and continue to pull the elastic through. When it comes full circle, fasten the ends together. Fig 5. Stitch the opening closed.

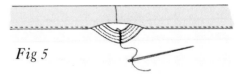

Fig 5

Closures

Rouleau loops are made from narrow cording or a long bias strip tube. The length should be sufficient to complete all the loops at once. The loops are positioned on the wrong side of the fabric, facing inwards and stitched across the ends of the loops to hold them in place. Fig 6. Pin the lining in position over the loops, turn the whole piece over and using the stitching as a guideline, stitch the lining in place. When the lining is turned back, the loops will extend beyond the finished edge. Fig 7. To create spaced out rouleau loops, cut the cording into short lengths and stitch separately. Pin and stitch lining as given above. Fig 8.

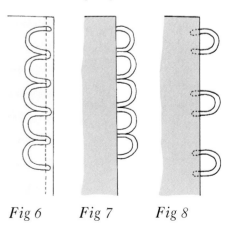

Fig 6   *Fig 7*   *Fig 8*

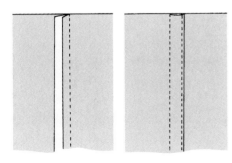

Fig 2   *Fig 3*

Snap fasteners are used where buttons would prove too bulky or where the area to be fastened is too small for a buttonhole to be worked. Using double thread, stitch through each hole of the snap three times and make sure the stitches do not show through to the right side of the garment.

Hooks and eyes should not be too large when making dolls clothes. A bar eye is preferable to the U-shaped eye as it gives a snug closure. Stitch in the loops and several times under the hook end. Fig 9.

Fig 9

A bar tack is used in place of an eye as it is delicate and inconspicuous. Work several taut stitches to form a bar and then work a close buttonhole stitch along the bar. Tie off at the back of the bar.

A buttonhole loop is used with a shank button. Work several loose stitches at the edge of the fabric where the loop will go. Pull the needle out at the base of the stitches and work a close buttonhole stitch round them for the whole length. When the loop is covered, fasten off the thread securely. Fig 10.

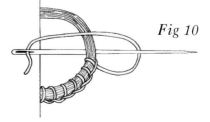

Fig 10

Glossary of stitches

Buttonhole stitch is a blanket stitch, worked very close together. Set the size and position of the buttonhole allowing for the thickness of the thread and mark with a faint pencil line. Using a single thread, run a line of small stitches round, and 3mm (⅛in) from, the pencil line. Fig 11.

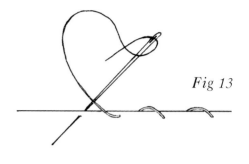

Fig 11

With small sharp scissors slash the pencil mark, knot the end of the thread and insert needle from front to back 12mm (½in) above the end of the buttonhole. Bring needle through the slash to front. To work small uniform buttonhole stitches, from the slash to the tacking line, insert the needle back between the slash, coming out at the lower edge of the tacking. Loop the thread from left to right, under the point of the needle and pull the needle up so that the loop forms directly on the slash. Fig 12. Complete the buttonhole, fasten the thread at the back and trim off original knot.

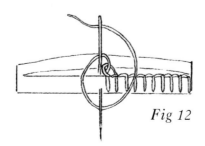

Fig 12

Whipstitch is used for attaching edging trims such as flat lace. With right sides together lay the trim along the edge of the fabric to which it is to

be joined. The two edges are stitched or whipped together. Open out the edging trim and press. Fig 13.

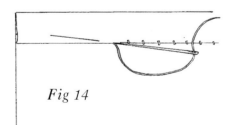

Fig 13

Hemstitch is a shorter version of whipstitch and is used for hemming.

Blind stitch is preferred to hemstitch when sewing small clothes and stitching hemlines. It is a neat and tidy stitch that will not pull out, unlike hemstitch. The needle travels under the folded edge of fabric coming up every 3mm (⅛in) to pick up a tiny stitch on the surface before going back under the folded edge. Fig 14.

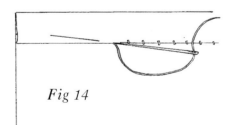

Fig 14

Overcasting If your machine does not have a zigzag stitch, use overcasting as an alternative to finishing a seam edge on fabrics that fray easily. It is a longer version of whipstitch. Fig 13. Make sure the edges of the fabric are trimmed of any ravelling threads before overcasting.

Stay stitch is a small running stitch worked within the seam allowance. It is used to keep the edge from pulling out of shape.

Basic Dressmaking Instructions

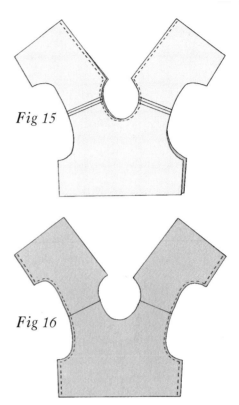

Fig 15

Fig 16

There are some basic dressmaking techniques that are common to several of the patterns in this book. Read them carefully and refer back to them as directed.

Interfacing

Iron-on interfacing, called Vilene, gives body and maintains the shape of the fabric pattern piece. Interfacing comes in different weights. Lightweight is recommended for waistbands, cuffs, facings, collars and anything that needs a small amount of body. Medium weight is recommended for hats and heavyweight for shoes. When fusing interfacing to fabric, gently steam press rather than ironing back and forth as this can stretch the fabric, especially when fusing to a bias cut piece such as a collar or hat brim.

Interfacing is pressed on to the wrong side of the fabric before the pattern piece is cut out unless otherwise stated. When a seam has been sewn, pull the interfacing away from the sewn edge and trim down to the line of stitching. This eliminates bulk when pressing the seam open.

Lining

Lining a garment gives a professional appearance. It gives a good finish to the neckline and sleeve openings, hides interfacing and adds body. A contrasting lining can add interest and style to a plain jacket whereas a pastel lining under

white broderie anglaise will show through the eyelets giving a lovely soft effect.

Use lightweight fabrics such as cotton lawn, batiste or self-fabric when lining other lightweight fabrics. If the fabric has a pattern sheer enough to see through, a lining of the same colour without a pattern should be used. Heavier materials such as velvet or wool should be lined with cotton or satin. Linings are often worked separately from the garments.

Frock bodices

Lining frock bodices gives a good finish to the neck area. The lining is usually worked separately.

Stitch bodice front and backs at shoulders and press seams open. Repeat for lining. (If the bodice has a collar, baste the finished collar to the bodice neckline and then sandwich the collar between the right sides of

the bodice and the lining.) Stitch the fabric and lining down the backs and around the neckline. Fig 15. Trim the corners; notch the neckline, turn and press. From this point the fabric and lining are worked as one piece. Stay stitch the lining to the bodice at the side front, around the sleeve openings and down the side back to keep them together. Fig 16. The side seams are stitched before or after the sleeves are set in depending on the method used.

When attaching the bodice to the skirt, complete the skirt and with right sides facing, pin skirt and bodice together, matching seams, or if the skirt is a dirndl, distributing the gathers evenly. Insert pins at right angles and stitch in place. Turn the raw edge up into bodice, press on the right side of garment, topstitch just above the seam line all the way around the waistline.

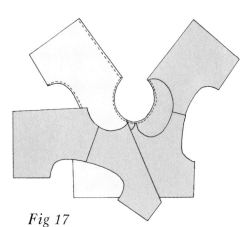

Fig 17

Collars

Make up the collar separately and then sew to the garment. The collar is always interfaced on one side. Use lightweight interfacing and iron on to the wrong side of the fabric. With right sides facing, stitch around collar leaving neck edge open. Trim, turn and press. With right sides facing, pin and baste the collar as a whole to the bodice neckline centring the back and matching any markings. Stitch in place. Fig 17. When the collar is complete the interfaced side should be on the top.

Setting in sleeves

Depending on the garment, sleeves can be made up by two different methods.

Method 1: A completed sleeve, which is set into a finished bodice.

Method 2: A sleeve, which is set into the bodice before the sleeve and side seams are sewn.

Measure the length from the doll's armpit and add the hem and seam allowance before cutting. When adding trim such as rickrack, braid or ribbon, stitch it on before the sleeve seam is stitched. Set the sleeve using one of the methods below and then turn up and stitch the hem.

Method 1
- With right sides facing, align sleeve to armhole, baste or pin in place distributing any gathers evenly.
- Stitch between the rows of gathering and pull out the gathering stitches.
- Trim the edges on fabrics that fray and neaten by overcasting.

Method 2
- Align sleeve to the armhole, baste or pin in place distributing any gathers evenly.
- Stitch between the rows of gathering and pull out the gathering stitches.
- With right sides facing stitch up the sleeve continuing down the bodice side seam.

Full sleeves are gathered at the wrist. Where you attach the elastic will depend on how much wrist ruffle you want.

Puffed sleeves are gathered above the elbow using shirring elastic (see page 11). Pull up the elastic to fit the doll's arm securing the other end when you stitch down the sleeve.

Straight sleeves must be wide enough to fit over the doll's hand.

Cuffs

To keep them crisp, cuffs are interfaced on one side of the length using lightweight iron-on Vilene. It is ironed lengthwise to the wrong side of the top half of the cuff.

Circular cuffs are cut to fit the sleeve end. Always make sure that they will

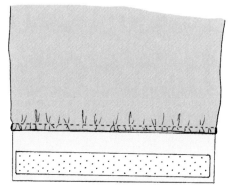

Fig 18

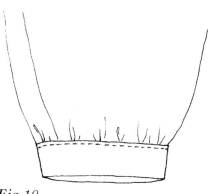

Fig 19

go over the doll's hand. With right side of non-interfaced cuff to wrong side of sleeve, stitch together and trim. Fig 18. The cuff and sleeve seam is sewn down the side and set as Method 1. Turn the cuff over the end of the sleeve, turn in the raw edge and topstitch in place. Fig 19. The interfaced side of the cuff should be on the outside of the sleeve.

Bound sleeve openings in sleeves are used with buttoned cuffs. Cut a slit in the sleeve end where indicated. Cut a strip of self-fabric on the bias, slightly longer than twice the length of the slit and 12mm (½in) wide. Press under 3mm (⅛in) on one side of the strip, spread the slit out horizontally and with right sides facing, pin the un-pressed edge of the strip to the edge of the slit. Stitch

Fig 23

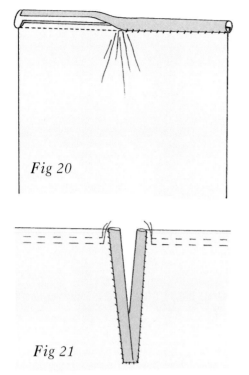

Fig 20

Fig 21

in place, pivoting the needle at the point. Take care not to stitch in any of the fullness of the sleeve. Fold the pressed edge of the strip over the raw sleeve edge and hand tack in place. Fig 20. Run gathering stitches around the sleeve opening, pull up gathers and set in cuff. Fig 21.

Buttoned cuffs are set each side of a gathered sleeve with a bound sleeve opening. With right sides together, fold the cuff in half lengthwise and stitch each end. Pin right side of

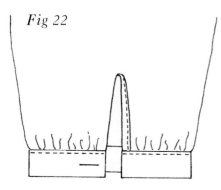

Fig 22

non-interfaced cuff to wrong side of sleeve end, pulling up gathers evenly, leaving an overlap at one end. Stitch in place. Turn the cuff over the sleeve end, turn in the raw edge and topstitch in place. Fig 22. Make buttonhole and sew on button.

Skirts

A skirt has a waistband or is sewn to a bodice. It can match the bodice or be of a contrasting colour. It can also be of a different fabric altogether such as a taffeta skirt with a velvet bodice. Skirts should be lined if the fabric is very lightweight or if it frays easily. The length is measured from the waist, adding seam and hem allowances. The hem is hand stitched.

For a skirt with waistband, cut the waistband twice the desired width plus seam allowance by the doll's waist measurement plus 12mm (1in). Iron on lightweight interfacing along one side of the length. With right sides facing, fold the waistband in half lengthwise and stitch across each end. Trim and turn to right side. Lay the interfaced side of the waistband against the skirt waist edge, right sides facing, and pin and stitch in place. The edge of the waistband is flush with the left side, with the extra 6mm (¼in) overlapping the right side of the skirt. Turn and press 6mm (¼in) along the raw edge of the waistband then turn it over the skirt edge and hand stitch in place. Make closures. Fig 23.

A flared skirt is made in panels and is fully lined. Match notches and stitch

all the seams and the back seam up to the opening. Work the lining separately. Press all seams open. With right sides of skirt and lining together, pin at hemline matching the seams. Stitch all the way around the hemline. Turn lining up and over the skirt and press hemline so that the lining does not show on the front of the skirt. Baste the lining to the skirt at the waistline, matching the seams, and stitch in place. Stay stitch around the back opening and attach the waistband. Make closures.

A dirndl skirt is a full skirt cut from a width of fabric three to four times the size of the doll's waistline, depending upon the weight of the fabric and the desired fullness. With right sides facing, stitch skirt together at back leaving a 5cm (2in) opening at the top. Run two parallel rows of gathering stitches, 6mm (¼in) apart around the top. Pull up the gathers, distributing them evenly, and with right sides together, pin skirt to bodice waistline or waistband matching centre of bodice/waistband to centre of skirt. Adjust the gathers and stitch between the rows. Remove bottom row of gathers, press seam up. Finish according to the pattern instructions.

The Victorian Collection

The doll shown is Queen Louise M102 a reproduction of an Armand Marseille German doll. She is 51cm (20in) high.

Instructions for making high-buttoned boots and a Merry Widow hat can be found in the Accessories section, pages 76 and 83.

to complete the look

Walking Out Costume

'While strolling through the park one day'

In the mid to late 1800s a costume for walking out was very fashionable. Waists were still corseted and jackets and skirts were smartly cut with almost a military feel. The trim was simple and the only frills were found at the neck and peeking out beneath the sleeves as a reminder of femininity. Large hats covered with plumage were the order of the day. While Nanny pushed the perambulator, the lady of the house was free to promenade with her husband while young ladies took the arms of their beaux.

This outfit fits a 51-56cm (20-22in) doll.

you will need

½ metre/yard velvet

½ metre/yard cotton lawn, silk or taffeta

Small amount of lace fabric, cotton lawn, silk or organza

Lightweight interfacing

1 metre/yard braid trim

25cm (10in) narrow silk cording

Shirring elastic

Narrow ribbon

5 shank buttons

1 button

Instructions

Engageantes
(half sleeves)

The sleeves shown are made from lace fabric with a broderie anglaise eyelet edging through which ribbon has been threaded and tied in a bow to create a cuff. If your fabric does not have eyelets, tie velvet ribbon around elasticized wrists once the garment is on the doll. Engageantes eliminate bulk under jackets on smaller dolls, but they could be replaced by an organza or silk Gibson girl blouse (page 36).

Pattern pieces required:
Engageantes 2D.

Cutting list: From lace fabric cut two 2D.

Making up
- Turn under raw edge at top and bottom of sleeves.
- If fabric does not have an eyelet edge stitch a trim to wrist edge and attach shirring elastic 2cm (¾in) above edge.
- Gather along the top edge.
- With right sides together, stitch side seams, making sure you don't catch the gathering stitches. Pull the shirring elastic up tight enough to fit doll's wrist, but loose enough to go over the hand. Secure the ends of the elastic.

Jacket

The waist-length jacket has three-quarter sleeves and no collar. It is fully lined and edged in braid trim

and fastens down the front with shank buttons and rouleau loops.

Pattern pieces required: Walking out jacket front 3C, Walking out jacket back 3D, Three-quarter sleeve 2I.

Cutting list: From velvet cut two 3C (one reversed), one 3D and two 2I. From lining cut two 3C (one reversed), one 3D and two 2I.

Making up
- Iron interfacing to jacket fronts.
- Work darts by folding along centre line and stitching along marked line. Press front darts towards side and back darts towards centre.
- Join at shoulders and sides. Repeat for lining.
- Make five rouleau loops along edge of front (see page 11). Try on doll to determine position.
- With right sides of jacket and lining together, stitch around the outside, sandwiching loops and leaving an opening at the bottom back for turning through. Turn to right side and stitch opening closed.

- With right sides together, stitch sleeve seam. Repeat for lining. Pull lining on to sleeve, right sides together, and stitch around wrist. Turn lining into sleeve and press so that it does not show. Baste together at shoulder. Repeat for the other sleeve.
- Turn sleeve inside out, slide engageantes (right side to lining), up to guideline, pull up gathers to fit, and stitch to lining. Do not let the stitches go through to catch

on the jacket sleeve fabric.

- Gather and set sleeves using Method 1 (see page 14).
- Measure all around the edge of the jacket for the braid, cut to length adding 12mm (½in) for seam allowance. Stitch the ends together, press and trim off the excess seam allowance. Matching braid seam with side seam of jacket, pin the braid around the edge and hand stitch in place.
- Sew on shank buttons to match rouleau loops.

Skirt

The skirt has an A-line flare made from five pieces. It is fully lined.

Pattern pieces required: Flared skirt front 3Q, Flared skirt back 3R and Flared skirt side 3S.

Cutting list: From velvet cut one 3Q, two 3R (one reversed), two 3S (one reversed), and a waistband 4.5cm (1¾in) wide by doll's waist measurement plus 2.5cm (1in). From lining cut one 3Q, two 3R (one reversed), and two 3S (one reversed).

Making up

- Matching marks, stitch fronts to sides and sides to back. Stitch back seam up to opening. Repeat for lining. Press seams open.
- With right sides of skirt and lining together, stitch at hemline and trim. Turn lining up and over skirt; making sure seams match. Press hemline so that lining does not show. Baste lining to skirt at waistline. Blind stitch lining to skirt each side of back opening.
- Set waistband (see page 15).
- Make buttonhole and sew on button to match.

Instructions for making a camisole, drawers and half-petticoat can be found in the Underclothes section, page 66.

what's underneath?

Adapt the Pattern
To create a calling costume, use a rustling brocade or raw silk fabric and lengthen the sleeves. Trim the neck, shoulder seams and cuff edge only. The skirt should be made fuller with petticoats worn underneath.

School Dress & Pinafore

*'School days, school days,
         dear old golden rule days.'*

Along sleeved dress with a pinafore over it was worn in the schoolroom by young girls in Victorian England. Under the dress were drawers and two petticoats, a full one made from cotton and another made from red flannel to give warmth in the chilly classroom. Sturdy black leather boots over black stockings, were the everyday wear of these little girls.

This outfit fits a 43-48cm (17-19in) doll.

The doll shown is a Dianna Effner design. She is 48cm (19in) high.

Instructions for making high-buttoned boots can be found in the Accessories section, page 80.

to complete the look

you will need

¼ metre/yard white poplin

¼ metre/yard black poplin

White bias binding

3 black buttons

1 white shank button

Instructions

Dress

The bodice is lined with self-fabric and buttons down the back. It has a Peter Pan collar, long straight sleeves and a dirndl skirt.

Pattern pieces required: Basic bodice front 1A, Basic bodice back 1B, Peter Pan collar 1L and Straight sleeve 1Z.

Cutting list: From black poplin cut two 1A, four 1B (two reversed), four 1L and two 1Z. For the dirndl skirt cut fabric width three times the doll's waist measurement by the required length plus hem and seam allowances.

Making up
- Interface two collar pieces before cutting out. With right sides together, stitch an interfaced collar to a non-interfaced collar leaving neck edge open. Clip, trim, turn out and press. Repeat for other collar.
- With right sides facing, stitch shoulder seams of bodice. Press open. Repeat for lining.
- Pin collar to right side of bodice and then, with right sides facing, stitch lining to bodice up backs and around neck, sandwiching collar. Trim, turn and press.
- Set in sleeves using Method 2 (see page 14).
- Make dirndl skirt and attach to bodice (see page 15).
- Make three buttonholes on bodice back and stitch on buttons to match.

Instructions for making drawers, petticoat, red flannel petticoat and long black stockings can be found in the Underclothes section, page 66.

Pinafore

This smock apron, with two patch pockets, is open at the back and fastened at the neck by one shank button. The gathered neckline incorporates a self-fabric ruffle and the armholes are bound with bias binding. There are two patch pockets.

Pattern pieces required: Pinafore front/back 2Q and Pinafore pocket 2P.

Cutting list: From white poplin cut two 2Q, two 2P and one yoke ruffle 71cm (28in) long by 10cm (4in) wide.

Making up
- Turn down 6mm (¼in) at the top of the pocket and stitch. With right sides facing, turn the top of the pocket over 12mm (½in) and stitch together at the sides. Clip the top corners.
- Run a single line of gathering stitches around the pocket from the turn down. Fig 1. Turn the pocket top right side out and press. Gently pull up the gathering stitches, turning the edges in smoothly, and press in place. Repeat for second pocket.
- Pin the completed pockets to the pinafore where indicated and topstitch in place.
- With right sides facing, stitch front and back together at shoulders. Press seams open.
- Turn in 6mm (¼in) down back edges and stitch in place. Turn in

Fig 1

WS

RS

another 6mm (¼in) and blind stitch by hand.

- Fold bias binding over raw edges of armholes and topstitch.
- With right sides together, fold ruffle in half lengthwise and stitch across both ends. Trim, turn right side out and press. Run gathering stitches along the length through both layers and pull up.
- Run gathering stitches around the neckline and pull up until the opening is about 28cm (11in). Concentrate the gathers at the front and back leaving the shoulder areas smooth.
- Pin the ruffle at the neckline adjusting the ruffle gathers evenly and stitch in place. Bind the neck edge with bias binding, turning in the ends, and topstitch.
- With right sides together stitch the side seams and press open.
- Turn up and stitch a 6mm (¼in) hem.
- Work a buttonhole loop (see page 12) at the top back neck under ruffle and sew on a shank button to match.

Adapt the Pattern

The Victorian school dress is easily adapted by replacing the straight sleeves with full sleeves with cuffs, eliminating the collar and adding button trim. An apron that ties at the back replaces the pinafore.

The doll shown is Twirp M1099, a French reproduction doll SFBJ 247 c.1915. He stands 56cm (22in) high.

Jack Tar Suit

*'I saw a ship a-sailing,
a-sailing on the sea'*

From the early 1800s right through to the 1930s, the sailor suit was the most popular and widely worn form of dress for young boys. The Jack Tar suit, named after the British sailor, was given added popularity by Queen Victoria's sons.

This outfit fits a 51-56cm (20-22in) doll.

Instructions for making high-buttoned boots and a sailor hat can be found in the Accessories section, pages 74 and 80.

to complete the look •

you will need

½ metre/yard navy wool serge

Small amount navy lining fabric

3 metre/yard white soutache braid

7 white buttons

46cm (18in) white ribbon

13cm (5in) elastic 2cm (¾in) wide

Lightweight Vilene

Nautical motif (optional)

Instructions

Tunic

The tunic style top has a round neckline, long sleeves and is fully lined. It buttons at the back and is tucked into bell-bottom trousers. The separate collar is interfaced and fastened at the front with a ribbon. Soutache braid trims the neckline, sleeves and collar.

Pattern pieces required: Jack Tar tunic front 3N, Jack Tar tunic back 3P, Jack Tar sleeve 2M and Sailor collar 1T.

Cutting list: From serge cut one 3N, two 3P (one reversed), two 2M and two 1T. From lining cut one 3N, two 3P (one reversed) and two 2M.

Making up
- Stitch front and backs together at the shoulders and down the sides. Repeat for lining.
- Topstitch two parallel rows of soutache braid to ends of sleeves and one row around the neck where indicated.
- With right sides facing, stitch the tunic and lining together around the outside leaving about 8cm (3in) open at the back for turning. Trim, turn, stitch the opening closed and press.
- With right sides together, stitch sleeve seams and press open. Set in sleeves using Method 1 (see page 14).
- Run gathering stitches at top of sleeve linings. With right sides facing, stitch seams and press open.
- With right sides facing push lining up into sleeve and stitch around wrist. Pull lining out and press seam open. Fig 1.
- With wrong sides facing, pull lining up sleeve, pull up gathers, turn in raw edge and blind stitch to bodice lining. Remove gathering stitches.
- Work buttonholes where indicated and sew on buttons to match.
- Sew on optional nautical motif to sleeve just below shoulder.

Sailor collar

Making up
- Iron interfacing to the wrong side of top collar.
- Stitch two rows of soutache braid to the right side of top collar where indicated.
- With right sides together, stitch around top and bottom collars, leaving the back neck open for turning through. Trim, turn and ease out corners.
- Stitch the opening closed and press.
- Work buttonhole loops at each end of the collar (see page 12). The collar is held together with ribbon passed through the loops and tied in a bow.

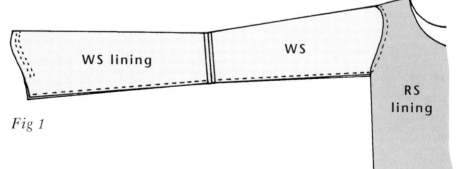

Fig 1

Bell-bottoms

The bell-bottom trousers are unlined with an elasticized back waist, side pockets and four decorative buttons. Some dolls have very large bottoms so be sure the elasticized waist will go over the hips.

Pattern pieces required: Bell-bottom front 3Z, Bell-bottom back 4A, Overall inner pocket 4B and Overall inner pocket lining 4C.

Cutting list: From serge cut two 3Z (one reversed), two 4A (one reversed), two 4B (one reversed), one front waistband 5cm (2in) wide by 18.5cm (7¼in) long and one back waistband 5cm (2in) wide by 20.5cm (8in) long. From lining cut two 4C (one reversed).

Making up

- With right sides facing, stitch fronts together from crotch to top. Trim, turn and press.
- Stitch inner pocket linings to fronts matching notches. Trim, turn, press and topstitch close to the edge.
- With right sides facing, stitch inner pockets to inner pocket linings matching notches. Overlock outside edge of pocket.

- With right sides facing, stitch backs together from crotch to top. Trim, turn and press.
- With right sides facing, stitch fronts to backs at the sides and inside legs. Press.
- With right sides facing, stitch front and back waistbands at the sides, stitching the elastic into the back band at each end at the same time. Fig 2.
- Stitch right side of waistband to right side of waist. Zigzag stitch or overcast the raw edges of the waist, then turn waistband over, turn edge 6mm (¼in) under and stitch in place.
- Zigzag stitch or overcast the leg openings, turn up 12mm (½in) hem and hand stitch.
- Sew on buttons, two on waistband and two below as shown. A nautical motif is optional.

Instructions for making combinations and long black stockings can be found in the Underclothes section, page 66.

Adapt the Pattern

For a summer sailor suit, shorten the trousers and use white duck or linen with a pale blue collar and navy trim. Or transform the outfit into a Skeleton Suit as shown above by lengthening the top of the trousers, tapering the legs and eliminating the sailor collar. Add a frill at the neckline and sew on lots of decorative buttons.

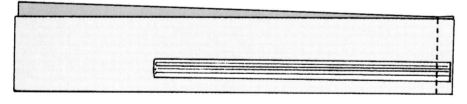

Fig 2

Sunday Best

*'Lavender's blue dilly, dilly,
lavender's green'*

The Sunday best dress was worn when attending church or visiting friends and relatives. On Sundays children were allowed out of the nursery to take tea in the drawing room with their parents. Sunday best also meant Sunday manners and children were not allowed to play in the garden as their clothes were easily spoiled. They played quietly with their Sunday toys – a special doll or a Noah's Ark. This Sunday dress has a nautical look with the overskirt drawn up to form panniers.

This outfit is designed to fit a 51-56cm (20-22in) doll.

The doll shown is Monica M1013, a reproduction of a German antique doll by C M Bergmann c.1916. She is 51cm (20in) high.

you will need

⅓ metre/yard blue calico

¼ metre/yard taffeta lining

Small amount of white calico

¼ metre/yard contrast colour calico

1 metre/yard satin ribbon 2cm (¾in) wide

1 metre/yard soutache braid

1 metre/yard small pompons
or about 30 individual pompons

Lightweight Vilene

4 buttons

to complete the look

Instructions for making ankle strap shoes can be found in the Accessories section, page 82.

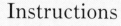

Instructions

Dress

The dress buttons down the back, has long flared sleeves, a dirndl skirt and detachable shawl collar. The collar and sleeves are trimmed with soutache braid. The bodice is lined but the sleeves are not.

Pattern pieces required: Basic bodice front 1A, Basic bodice back 1B, Shawl collar 1M and Flared sleeve 2A.

Cutting list: From blue calico cut two 1A, four 1B (two reversed) and two 2A. From white calico cut two 1M. From contrast calico cut a dirndl skirt four times the doll's waist measurement by skirt length plus hem and seam allowances.

Making up
- Work the bodice and lining as in frock bodices (see page 13).
- Stitch soutache braid on sleeves where indicated. With right sides facing, stitch sleeve seams and set in sleeves using Method 1 (see page 14).
- The shawl collar is separate from the bodice.
- Iron interfacing to the wrong side of top collar.
- Stitch a row of soutache braid to the right side of top collar where indicated.
- With right sides together, stitch around top and bottom collars, leaving the back neck open for turning through. Trim, turn and ease out corners.
- Stitch the opening closed and press.

- Make buttonhole loops (see page 12) at both ends of the collar large enough for one of the buttons to pass through.
- Work dirndl skirt (see page 15) and stitch to bodice. Sew a button to the centre front of the bodice where it meets the skirt. When the collar is placed around the doll's neck, the buttonhole loops fasten around the button to secure it.
- Work three buttonholes at the back of the bodice and sew on buttons to match.

Pannier

The pannier is a separate flounced overskirt that ties in a bow at the back. It is made from calico and lined with taffeta.

Pattern piece required: Pannier 3V.

Cutting list: From blue calico cut one 3V and one waistband 4.5cm (1¾in) by doll's waist measurement plus 12mm (½in). From taffeta cut one 3V.

Making up
- If you are using a length of pompons, sandwich them between the pannier and the lining before stitching. If you are using individual pompons, stitch them on by hand after the pannier and lining have been stitched together.
- With right sides facing, stitch pannier and lining together leaving top open. Trim, turn and press.
- Divide pannier into three even sections and mark with a line of

Instructions for making a petticoat, drawers, and long white stockings can be found in the Underclothes section, page 66.

what's underneath?

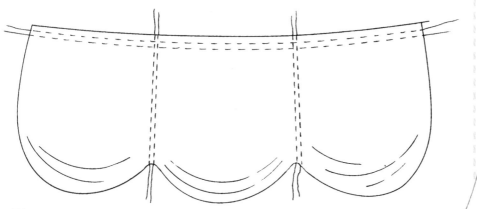

Fig 1

loose running stitch. This is where you will gather up the flounces.

- To create the flouncing, start at the bottom of the pannier and, with tiny stitches, sew two lines of gathering up to the waistband along the lines of running stitch. Remove running stitches, pull up gathers and fasten off securely on the underside. Fig 1.
- Run gathering stitches along the top of the pannier and attach to the waistband distributing the gathers evenly to each end of the band (see page 15).
- Pin satin ribbon around waistband, leaving 30.5cm (12in) at either end for ties. Topstitch along top and bottom edges of ribbon. Tie ends at the back
- Tie a bow with the remaining ribbon and stitch it to the front of the waistband.

Adapt the Pattern

The Sunday dress can be turned into an afternoon day dress for an older girl by dropping the hemline to the floor, trimming the edges of the sleeves, collar and hem with lace and tying a big bow around the waist.

Travelling Coat and Spatterdashes

'To travel hopefully is a better thing than to arrive'

Whether travelling by train or a short journey by omnibus, children were always dressed for the occasion. Animal fur was widely used at this time, for children as well as adults, and rabbit fur was particularly fashionable for children's wear. Long pile mohair gives an authentic look for the style of the day. Spatterdashes kept little legs warm and clean. They reached from above the knee and extended over the top of the shoe.

This outfit is designed for a 43-48cm (17-19in) doll.

The doll shown is a reproduction of a German Barnaby doll made by The Dolls House. The face has been painted in modern style. She is 48cm (19in) high.

Instructions for making a Glengarry bonnet and Mary Jane shoes are found in the Accessories section, pages 74 and 80.

to complete the look

you will need

¼ metre/yard lightweight wool

¼ metre/yard cotton lining

Lightweight Vilene

Small amount of long pile mohair fabric

Bias tape and elastic

8 snap fasteners

3 buttons

12 tiny buttons

Instructions

Coat

The simple A-line design buttons down the front. The collar and cuffs are made from pink mohair to match the coat and lined with cotton fabric.

Pattern pieces required: Travelling coat front 3E, Travelling coat back 3K, Basic sleeve 1X, Mohair collar 1U and Mohair cuff 2L.

Cutting list: From wool cut two 3E (one reversed), one 3K and two 1X. From cotton lining cut two 3E (one reversed) and one 3K 6mm (¼in) shorter than the coat, two 1X 12mm (½in) shorter than the sleeves and one 1U. From mohair cut one 1U and two 2L. (Before cutting out fur fabric see page 9.)

Making up

- With right sides facing, stitch back and fronts together at shoulders. Press seams open. Repeat for lining.
- Work and set in sleeves using Method 1 (see page 14). Repeat for lining.
- With right sides facing, stitch around the fur collar and lining leaving the neck edge open. Trim, turn to right side and comb out any trapped fur. Pin the collar to the right side of the neckline and baste in place.
- With right sides facing, pin the lining to the coat, sandwiching the collar and stitch around the neckline and down the front openings. Trim, turn and press.
- Turn the coat sleeves up to hang just below the doll's wrist and hand stitch in place. Turn linings up 6mm (¼in) shorter than sleeves. Push the sleeve linings up into the sleeves and turn the coat and sleeves right side out. Blind stitch the sleeve linings to the sleeves.
- Stitch bias tape to coat hem. Turn up over lining and hand hem.
- Stitch fur cuffs together at ends. Trim and comb out any trapped fur from seams. Pull the cuff over the sleeve, turn in the raw edges and hand stitch to sleeve at top and bottom of cuff.
- Work buttonholes on front of coat and sew on buttons to match.

Spatterdashes

These leggings fasten up the side with snap fasteners under decorative buttons. They are made in the same wool fabric as the coat.

Pattern pieces required: Spatterdash inside 5W, Spatterdash outside front 5X and Spatterdash outside back 5Y.

Cutting out: From wool cut two 5W (one reversed), two 5X (one reversed) and two 5Y (one reversed).

Making up

- Iron on interfacing before cutting out pieces. Note that the seam allowance is 3mm (⅛in).
- With right sides facing, stitch inside to outside front matching notches.
- Stitch inside to outside back matching notches.
- Press seams open and run a small close zigzag stitch twice around the outside edge. Carefully trim the edge of the zigzag stitching.
- Outside front closes over the outside back with four snap fasteners on each spatterdash. Sew six tiny buttons at regular intervals on top.

Adapt the Pattern

The travelling coat can be adapted to a short jacket using lightweight worsted fabric. Hem the jacket just above the hipline, leave the sleeves long and eliminate the collar. Without overlapping the front, stitch hooks and eyes on the undersides to form an invisible closure. Add patch pockets.

The Edwardian Collection

*The doll shown is a reproduction of the 1910
French doll, Mon Cheri Paris c.1910,
M1004. She is 45.5 (18in) high.*

Instructions for making a motoring bonnet and
high-buttoned boots can be found in the
Accessories section, pages 74 and 80.

to complete the look •

Motoring Wear
for a Gibson Girl

*'Come away with me Lucile,
in my merry Oldsmobile,
Down the road of life we'll fly,
automo-bubbling you and I'*

With the birth of the motorcar, protective clothing was essential. Cars had no windscreens or doors, and the roads were not yet tarmaced so it was a dusty business. Leather, gabardine and animal fur was worn by the very wealthy, but coats made from heavy cotton fabric, called dusters, were easily laundered and proved very popular with the average motorist. The American artist Charles Gibson immortalized the women of his day, giving them a haughty look and wearing their hair piled up on their head. This Gibson girl wears a blouse with a pretty lace-edged jabot and a skirt to match her coat.

This outfit is designed for a 43-48cm (17-19in) doll.

you will need

½ metre/yard cotton broadcloth

½ metre/yard cotton lining

8 buttons covered with self fabric

4 snap fasteners

1 button

Bias tape

Remnant of silk or cotton lawn

Length of narrow lace

Small amount of cotton batiste

Instructions

Duster

This three-quarter-length coat has a round collar, long sleeves that puff at the top and two patch pockets. A back yoke conceals a welt and has a decorative tab. The coat is completely lined and buttons down the front with covered buttons. There are matching buttons on the sleeves and tab. Follow the manufacturer's instructions for covering the buttons.

Pattern pieces required: Duster front 3E, Duster side back 3F, Duster centre back 3G, Duster yoke 3H, Basic sleeve 1X, Duster collar 1S, Duster front facing 3I, Duster neck facing 3J, Duster pocket 3L, Duster tab 3M, Duster back lining 3K.

Cutting list: From broadcloth cut two 3E, two 3F, one 3G, two 3H, two 1X, two 1S, two 3I (one reversed), one 3J, two 3L and two 3M. From lining cut two 3E, one 3K and two 1X.

Making up

- With right sides facing, stitch centre back to side backs matching notches. Press seams towards the sides.
- Fold side backs back over centre back to form a welt. Fig 1. Press welt and baste top edge.
- Sandwich basted edge of backs between yokes and stitch in place. Fig 2. Turn yokes up, press and topstitch in place. Fig 3.
- Stitch down 6mm (¼in) at the top of pocket. With right sides facing, turn the top of pocket over 12mm

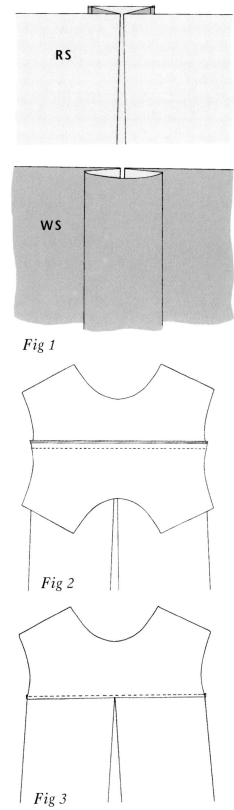

RS

WS

Fig 1

Fig 2

Fig 3

(½in) and stitch together at sides. Clip the corners and turn to right side. Topstitch across the pocket to hold the turned edge in place. Turn the remaining edges in 6mm (¼in) and press. Pin the completed pockets to the duster where indicated and topstitch in place.

- Stitch fronts to yoke at shoulders. Press seams up and topstitch.

- Stitch side seams and press open.
- Set in sleeves using Method 1 (see page 14). Turn 6mm (¼in) hem at sleeve ends and topstitch in place.
- Stitch bias tape to hemline of duster, turn up and hand hem. Press.
- Stitch lining fronts and back together at shoulders. Stitch side seams.
- Set in sleeves as for duster.
- With wrong sides facing, match lining to duster, pushing sleeve linings into the sleeves. Blind stitch all around.
- Work and set collar (see page 14).
- Stitch back and front facings together and press seams open. Turn in outer raw edge and stitch. Press.
- With wrong sides facing, pin facing over collar at neckline and down front sides. Stitch in place. Trim, turn, press and hand tack to lining only.
- With right sides facing, stitch around tab leaving opening for turning through. Turn to right side, fold opening in, press and topstitch all around. Set about 3.5cm (1½in) down from yoke and stitch in place with two buttons.
- Work buttonholes down front and stitch buttons to match. Sew buttons on sleeves.

Jabot

This lace-edged dickey is stitched into the collar at the centre front of the blouse.

Pattern piece required: Jabot 3W.

Cutting list: From silk/cotton batiste cut two 3W.

Making up
- If the lace is not already ruffled, gather by hand and pull up to fit around jabot.
- Pin the gathered lace around the edge with the lace facing inwards. Baste in place.
- With right sides facing, stitch the lining over the jabot leaving the top open for turning. Trim, turn and press gently.

Blouse

Fastened down the back with snap fasteners, the blouse has long full sleeves that gather into cuffs. The stand-up collar is accentuated by a lace-edged jabot. The blouse is not lined but both the collar and cuffs are interfaced.

Pattern pieces required: Gibson blouse front 5F, Gibson blouse back 5G, Gibson sleeve 2H.

Cutting list: From cotton batiste cut one 5F, two 5G (one reversed), two 2H, one collar 5cm (2in) wide by 20.5cm (8in) long and two cuffs 5cm (2in) wide by doll's wrist measurement plus 2cm (¾in). (Make sure cuff will go over doll's hand.)

Making up
- With right sides facing, stitch front and backs together at shoulders. Press seams open.
- Run gathering stitches at the top and bottom of sleeves.
- With right sides facing, stitch sleeve seams. Cut a slit in the sleeve where indicated and follow the instructions for bound openings (see page 15).
- Set in sleeves using Method 1 (see

Instructions for making a camisole, bloomers, long stockings and a half-petticoat can be found in the Underclothes section, page 66.

What's underneath?

page 14) and work buttoned cuffs.

- With right sides facing, fold collar in half lengthwise and stitch ends closed. Trim, turn and press.
- Turn in 3mm (⅛in) along raw edge of centre backs then turn in a further 2cm (¾in) and press.
- Pin the top edge of the jabot to the centre front of the blouse and, with right sides facing, pin the back of the collar to the neckline and stitch in place. Turn front of collar over and hand stitch around neckline.
- Work snap fasteners at the back and the cuffs.
- Zigzag or overcast the bottom edge of the blouse, turn up 6mm (¼in) and stitch in place.

Skirt

The full-length skirt is made from five panels that flare out at the hemline. It is fully lined with a waistband that buttons at the back.

Pattern pieces required: Flared skirt front 3Q, Flared skirt back 3R and Flared skirt side 3S.

Cutting out: From broadcloth and lining cut one 3Q, two 3R, two 3S and from broadcloth only, one waistband 5cm (2in) wide by doll's waist measurement plus 2.5cm (1in).

Making up
- With right sides together and matching notches, stitch all seams in front, sides and back panels leaving back seam open from indication. Repeat for lining. Press seams open.
- With right sides facing, stitch skirt and lining together at hemline.

Trim, turn lining up and over skirt, making sure seams are matching. Press hemline so that lining does not show. Baste lining to skirt at waistline. Blind stitch lining to skirt around opening.
- Attach waistband (see page 15).
- Make buttonhole and stitch on button to match.

Adapt the Pattern

Make the duster without the pockets into a fur coat. Use imitation animal fur like mink or leopard with a velveteen collar to eliminate bulk – or leave off the collar altogether. A Glengarry bonnet makes a matching hat. For a more feminine look try taffeta for the skirt teamed with an organza blouse over a chemisette. Gather the sleeves of the blouse at the wrist and work a pin-tucked bodice trimmed with lace and ribbon.

The doll shown is a Dianna Effner design. She is 48cm (19in) high.

Instructions for making Mary Jane shoes can be found in the Accessories section, page 80. Straw hats in various sizes are available in craft stores and doll shops. Stitch ribbon around the edge of the hat brim and around the crown, crossing at the back.

Sailor Dress

'By the sea, by the sea,
by the beautiful sea!'

First in tunics and then in dresses, girls adapted the ever-popular sailor style generally worn by boys. The classic collar, braid trim and dickey have been modified and elaborated on over the years, according to the dictates of fashion and to suit the age and gender of the child, but the sailor style always remains recognizable.

This outfit fits a 43-48cm (17-19in) doll.

you will need

½ metre/yard cotton duck or linen

Cotton lining fabric

1 metre/yard soutache braid

3 buttons

46cm (18in) satin ribbon

Bias tape

Lightweight Vilene

2 star motifs (optional)

Instructions

Sailor dress

The lined bodice, which buttons at the back, has a low waistline attached to an unlined box pleated skirt. The separate collar is interfaced and lined with self-fabric. Soutache braid trims the neckline, sleeves and collar and a big satin bow ties the collar together.

Pattern pieces required: Sailor dress bodice front 1J, Sailor dress bodice back 1K, Tapered sleeve 2K and Sailor collar 1T.

Cutting list: From cotton duck cut one 1J, two 1K (one reversed), two 2K, two 1T and one skirt panel 114cm (45in) long by 18cm (7in) deep. From cotton lining cut one 1J and two 1K (one reversed).

Making up

- Work box pleats on the skirt panel (see box below).
- Stitch the centre back seam up to the opening and press the seam open.
- Stitch the front and back bodices together at shoulders. Press seams open. Repeat for lining. Run a zigzag stitch or overcast around the sleeve openings of the lining only.
- Stitch a row of soutache braid to sleeves and neckline where shown.
- Fold bias tape over raw edges of sleeve ends and topstitch in place.
- Set in sleeves using Method 2 (see page 14).
- With right sides facing, stitch lining to bodice around neckline and down backs. Trim, turn and press.
- Stitch lining to sleeve openings at bottom.
- Pin lining and bodice together at the bottom raw edge and zigzag to finish.
- With right sides facing, attach pleated skirt to bodice. Press seam allowance up and topstitch in place.
- If your hemline is not a woven edge, run a zigzag stitch or overcast along the raw edge, turn up 6mm (¼in) and topstitch in place. Steam press pleats back into position.
- Work buttonholes on bodice and sew on buttons to match.

Sailor collar

Making up

- Stitch braid on the interfaced collar piece using the guideline closest to the edge. With right sides facing, stitch around the collar pieces, leaving the back neck open for turning. Trim and turn out.
- Slipstitch opening closed and press.
- Work buttonhole loops at each end of the collar (see page 12). Run satin ribbon through the loops and tie in a bow to close.

Instructions for making a liberty bodice and bloomers can be found in the Underclothes section, page 66.

What's underneath?

Box pleats

A 2.5cm (1in) pleat takes 7.5cm (3in) of fabric. Measure and mark your fabric at 2.5cm (1in) intervals. Add fabric to allow for the back seam.

Making up

- Mark the fold lines with tailor's chalk and pin the pleats at the top, centre and bottom. When all the pleats are completed, run basting stitches across the three points where the pleats are pinned. Fig 1.
- Carefully steam press the pleats in place making sure they are all even and that the back seam will be concealed under a pleat, adjust if necessary. Steam both sides of the fabric until the pleats are crisp.
- Stitch across the top of the skirt to hold the pleats and take out the basting stitches.

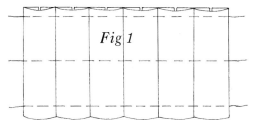

Fig 1

Adapt the Pattern

Turn the dress into a pretty party outfit by shortening the sleeves, adding rows of ruffles, one at the neckline, two on the sleeves and three wide rows on a skirt made from a panel of fabric. Stitch ruffles on to the skirt before making up and attaching to the bodice.

The doll used is an Elise doll. He stands 61cm (24in) high.

Instructions for making a peak cap and Balmoral boots can be found in the Accessories section, pages 74 and 80.

to complete the look •

Norfolk Suit

'In the good ol' summer time'

Country tweeds and jaunty cloth caps were popular wear for sporting activities and travelling before the coming of the motorcar. Little boys of well-to-do families were often dressed as miniature versions of their fathers and the Norfolk jacket was a favourite with its belted waistline and box pleats.

This outfit fits a 58-63.5cm (23-25in) doll.

you will need

½ metre/yard lightweight worsted wool

¼ metre/yard contrasting cotton fabric

¼ metre/yard cotton poplin

7 covered buttons in self-fabric

7 buttons

4 buttons

12mm (½in) wide black elastic

26cm (10in) thin black cord or black shirring elastic

Lightweight Vilene

Jacket and belt

The belted jacket has a collar and straight sleeves. There are two box pleats at the front, side panels under the arms, and self-covered buttons.

Pattern pieces required: Norfolk front 2X, Norfolk side panel 2Y, Norfolk back 2Z, Norfolk front lining 3A, Norfolk back lining 3B, Norfolk collar 1Q and Norfolk sleeve 2E.

Cutting list: From wool cut two 2X (one reversed), two 2Y (one reversed), one 2Z, two 1Q and a belt 7.5cm (3in) by doll's waist measurement plus 9cm (3½in) overlap. From lining cut two 3A (one reversed), one 3B and two 2E.

Making up
- Make box pleats in jacket by folding along guidelines. On the wrong side of the box pleat, stitch the vent closed with a long running stitch.
- Steam press the box pleats and topstitch them on either side. Fig 1.
- Iron interfacing to fronts and back neck where indicated.
- With right sides facing, stitch jacket fronts and back at shoulders.
- With right sides facing, stitch side panels to fronts and back matching notches. Press all seams open.
- With right sides facing, stitch front and back linings at shoulders and side seams. Press seams open.
- Make and set collar (see page 14).
- With right sides facing, stitch lining to jacket sandwiching collar. Trim, turn to right side and press.
- With right sides facing, stitch sleeve seams. Repeat for linings.

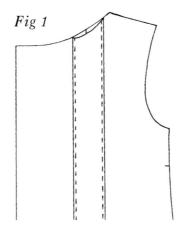

Fig 1

Run gathering stitches at the top of sleeves and linings.
- With right sides facing, pull the lining on to sleeve and stitch around wrist. Trim, turn lining into sleeve and press so the lining ends 6mm (¼in) up the sleeve.
- Set in sleeve (not sleeve lining) using Method 1 (see page 14), matching the indication marks on the sleeves to the indication marks on the jacket backs. Turn the raw edge of the sleeve linings in and, easing fullness by pulling up the gathers, hand stitch to the jacket lining. Remove gathering stitches.
- Turn up a 12mm (½in) hem along bottom of jacket over the lining. Turn the front facings over the interfacing and hand stitch in place. Press.
- Iron interfacing lengthways to half of the belt. With wrong sides facing, fold belt in half lengthways and stitch to form a curved edge one end and along long edge. Trim, turn, press and stitch opening closed.
- Cover buttons with self-fabric following maker's instructions.
- Try the jacket on the doll with the belt around the waist to decide where the buttons will go. Work two buttonholes above the belt, one below and two on the belt as shown. Stitch on buttons to match.

Knickerbockers

There are two tucks at the front below the waistband and the legs gather into buttoned cuffs below the knees. The waistband and cuffs are interfaced. If your doll has a hard body, the waist will be smaller than the hips. Set elastic into the back of the waistband following instructions on page 26. The knickerbockers will squeeze over a cloth body to fit.

Pattern pieces required: Knickerbockers front 3X and Knickerbockers back 3Y.

Cutting list: From wool cut two 3X (one reversed), two 3Y (one reversed), one waistband 5cm (2in) wide by doll's waist measurement plus seam allowance and two leg bands 5cm (2in) by doll's leg measurement plus 4cm (1½in) overlap.

Making up

- With right sides facing, stitch fronts from crotch to waist and backs from crotch to waist. Clip and press seams open.
- Match point A to point B on the front and, on the wrong side of fabric, form a tuck by stitching down about 2.5cm (1in). Turn tucks toward the centre, baste and press in place.
- With right sides facing stitch fronts and backs together at sides and from waist to indication mark. Press seams open and tack around leg openings. Fig 2. Run a row of gathering stitches at bottom of legs.
- With right sides together, fold leg cuffs in half lengthways and stitch across both ends, leaving the bottom edge open. Trim, turn and press.
- Pin right side of cuff to wrong side of pant leg pulling up the gathers evenly and leaving a 4cm (1½in) overlap towards the back. Stitch, fold cuff over the outside of the pant leg, turn the raw edge down 6mm (¼in) and topstitch in place.

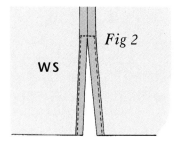

WS

Fig 2

Fitted shirt

The shirt nips in at the waist and has a shirt tail, French cuffs that fold back to fasten with a button cufflink and a stand-up collar. The shirtfronts form the front facing. Run and fell seams (see page 11) are used at the shoulders, sleeves and sides of the shirt.

Pattern pieces required: Fitted shirt front 5C, Fitted shirt back 5D, Fitted shirt sleeve 2N, French cuff 2G, Fitted shirt collar 1R, Fitted shirt neck facing 5E.

Cutting list: From poplin cut two 5C (one reversed), one 5D, two 2N, four 2G, two 1R and one 5E.

Making up

- With right sides facing, stitch fronts and back together at shoulders.
- Work and attach collar (see page 14).
- Stitch neck facing to ends of front facings. Press seams open and turn in 6mm (¼in) all around the outside edge of facing. Press.
- With right sides facing, turn facing over and with collar sandwiched between facing and shirt, stitch together. Trim, turn and press.
- Work and set sleeves using Method 2 (see page 14).
- Make sleeve bound openings and set in cuff (see pages 14 and 15).
- Turn up and stitch a 6mm (¼in) hem around the bottom of the shirt.
- Work five buttonholes down front, including one on collar, and each cuff. Sew on buttons to match.

Braces

Made from lengths of wide black elastic, the braces are sewn to the back of the trousers and attached to buttons at the front.

Making up

- Turn one end of the elastic up 12mm (½in) and stitch in place.
- Cut 5cm (2in) from fabric cord and feed it through the stitched end of the elastic. Stitch ends together to make a loop.
- Repeat for second brace.

- Try the trousers on your doll to determine where the braces should be stitched at the back and pin in place. Cross and pin the braces where they cross at the back. Mark where the buttons should be placed on the front waistband.
- Take the trousers and braces off the doll and stitch the braces to the trousers at the inside back. Take a few stitches at the point where they cross.
- Stitch buttons to the trouser fronts where marked. The loops of the cord fit around the buttons.

what's underneath?

Instructions for making combinations and black ribbed stockings can be found in the Underclothes section, page 66.

Adapt the Pattern

The Norfolk suit easily adapts to a Little Lord Fauntleroy suit by cuffing the sleeves, losing the box pleats, adding lace trim to the collar, narrowing the belt and replacing its buttons with a buckle. Leave the cuffs off the ends of the pair of knickerbockers.

Nightdress

'In winter I get up at night
and dress by yellow candlelight,
In summer quite the other way,
I have to go to bed by day'

A mug of hot cocoa and snuggling up in a big feather bed on a cold wintry night with a favourite doll and a good storybook was how Victorian children ended the day. A full-length flannel nightdress was worn in winter, replaced by a cotton version in summer.

This outfit is designed for a 43–48cm (17–19in) doll.

you will need

½ metre/yard white cotton lawn

1½ metre/yard of 12mm (½in) eyelet lace

1½ metre/yard of 12mm (½in) satin ribbon

Shirring elastic

2 snap fasteners

The doll shown is from the author's collection. She is 43cm (17in) high.

Instructions for making a mob cap and carpet slippers can be found in the Accessories section, pages 74 and 80.

to complete the look •

Instructions

Nightdress

The embroidered nightdress with full length sleeves is made from white cotton lawn and buttons down the back. The front bodice is pintucked and edged with eyelet lace and satin ribbon. Lace is also sewn around the neckline and there is a self-ruffle trimmed with more eyelet lace and ribbon at the hem. The pintucks and embroidery are worked before the bodice is cut out. Pintucks are not difficult, but the measuring is very precise, so work slowly and carefully.

Pattern pieces required: Nightdress bodice front 1E, Nightdress bodice back 1F and Basic sleeve 1X.

Cutting list: From pintucked fabric cut one 1E, from cotton cut one 1E, four 1F (two reversed), two 1X, one skirt 68.5cm (27in) wide by a minimum length of 28cm (11in). Cut a skirt ruffle 6.5cm (2½in) wide by 137cm (54in) long.

Adapt the Pattern

The Victorian nightdress is easily transformed into a party dress by shortening the length of the skirt and shortening the sleeves. Add lace and ribbon at the neck and sleeves and replace the bodice ruffle with a wide satin sash that ties at the back in a big bow.

Pintucks

- Cut a rectangle of fabric three times wider than the pattern piece you are working on. With wrong sides facing, and working from the centre, fold the fabric where you want the first pintuck to go and steam press in place.
- With the folded edge at the top, use a ruler to lightly pencil a 5mm (³⁄₁₆in) line below the fold. Stitch directly on this guideline when sewing the pintuck. Steam press the tuck down, pulling gently at the fabric to create a tight tuck. The pencil mark will now be underneath.
- To make the second pintuck, turn the fabric to the wrong side and press again. Measure from the stitching line down 1.5cm (⅝in). Fold fabric up and under and press in place.
- Follow the instructions for the first tuck drawing a line 5mm (³⁄₁₆in) below the fold. When you have completed the tucks on one side, turn the fabric and work tucks in the opposite direction. Centre the pattern over the fabric and cut out.

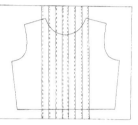

Making up

- Stitch the pintucked bodice front to the bodice backs at shoulders. Press seams open. Repeat for lining.
- Pin eyelet lace around neckline.
- Stitch bodice lining to bodice down the back and around the neck sandwiching the eyelet lace in between. Turn and press.
- Run gathering stitches or shirring elastic at ends of sleeves. Work and set sleeves using Method 2 (see page 14).
- With right sides facing, fold skirt in half and stitch together leaving a 5cm (2in) opening at the top. Press seam open and run a line of stitching around the skirt opening to neaten.
- With right sides facing, stitch short ends of ruffle together to form a loop. Press seam open. With wrong sides together fold in half lengthways and press. Gather raw edges of ruffle and, with right sides facing, pin ruffle to bottom of skirt matching raw edges and pulling up gathers to fit. Stitch in place, press seam allowance up

into skirt and topstitch.

- Stitch eyelet lace over the top of the skirt ruffle and hand stitch satin ribbon on top, starting off centre front and leaving 10cm (4in) of ribbon free. Tie a bow at the end.
- Run gathering stitches at top of skirt and stitch to bodice distributing the gathers evenly.
- Topstitch lace around edge of bodice turning in the ends.
- Hand stitch narrow satin ribbon over the lace edge at the bodice and hem. Add bows or flowers.
- Work two snap fasteners or buttonholes at the back.

Lazy Daisy Stitch
The lazy daisy is commonly used to make leaf and petal stitches. The needle is pulled up through the fabric, looped on the surface and held down with the thumb while the needle is pushed back through the same hole and up through the top of the loop securing it with a single stitch.

Faux Fur Suit

*'Daisy, Daisy,
Give me your answer do'*

As women were freed from the tight hourglass look of the corset, the loose fitting suit, like this one made from wool worsted, gave a stylish line to the newly liberated woman. The jacket is trimmed with a beautiful fur collar and matching muff. A silk chemisette worn under the jacket gives a feminine look.

This outfit is designed for a 58-63.5cm (23-25in) doll.

The doll shown is a reproduction of the German Mein Liebling (My Darling). She stands 61cm (24in) high.

you will need

½ metre/yard lightweight worsted wool

½ metre/yard silk or cotton batiste lining fabric

½ metre/yard imitation fur fabric

Small amount of silk

2 snap fasteners

1 button

Seam binding

to complete the look •

Instructions for making a wide brim cloche hat and high-buttoned boots can be found in the Accessories section, see pages 74 and 80.

Jacket

The jacket is lined with silk, but you could use cotton batiste. It has long straight sleeves and a deep V-neck with a fur collar that overlaps at the front. Two snap fasteners secure the jacket.

Pattern pieces required: Faux fur collar 1P, Straight suit sleeve 2C, Faux fur jacket front 2V and Faux fur jacket back 2W.

Cutting list: From wool cut two 2V (one reversed), one 2W, and two 2C. From lining fabric cut two 2V (one reversed), one 2W, two 2C, and one 1P. From fur cut two 1P (one reversed). Before cutting the fur see page 9.

Making up

- With right sides facing stitch centre back of jacket, then join back to front at shoulders and down sides. Press all seams open. Repeat for lining.
- Stitch sleeve seams and press open. Repeat for lining.
- With right sides facing pull lining on to sleeve and stitch around sleeve end. Turn lining into sleeve and press so it does not show.
- Set sleeves into jacket using Method 1 (see page 14).
- With right sides facing, stitch fur collar together at back, then with right sides facing, stitch collar and lining together all around, leaving an opening at the back neck edge for turning. Trim, turn to right side, stitch opening and comb out any trapped fur.
- Blind stitch to attach the collar

around neck and along the front edge of jacket. Secure lower edge of collar at centre back with a few stitches.
- Sew snap fasteners where indicated to fasten.

Skirt

The full-length skirt has a waistband that buttons at the back. It is fully lined with the lining worked separately.

Pattern pieces required: Straight skirt front 3T and Straight skirt back 3U.

Cutting list: From wool cut one 3T, two 3U (one reversed), and one waistband 5cm (2in) wide by doll's waist measurement plus 4cm (1½in). From lining fabric cut one 3T and two 3U (one reversed).

Making up

- Stitch darts in front and back, starting at the widest part and running the stitching off the tip and knotting the thread. Press towards sides. Repeat for lining.
- With right sides facing, stitch side seams and back seam to mark. Press seams open. Repeat for lining.
- Stitch seam binding to skirt hemline.
- Baste lining inside skirt at waistline.
- Blind stitch lining to skirt around back opening.
- Attach waistband to skirt (see page 15). Make buttonhole and sew on button to match.
- Turn bottom of skirt up and hand stitch hem. Hem lining separately on machine.

Instructions for making a camisole, drawers and long black stockings can be found in the Underclothes section, page 66.

What's underneath?

Chemisette

The chemisette is a sleeveless and collarless shell that fastens at the back. It is made from silk with a self lining.

Pattern pieces required: Chemisette front 4N and Chemisette back 4M.

Cutting list: From silk cut two 4N and four 4M (two reversed).

Making up
- With right sides facing, stitch bodice front and bodice backs together at shoulders. Press seams open. Repeat for lining.
- With right sides of bodice and lining facing, stitch around neck opening, down the backs and around armholes. Trim, turn and press.
- With right sides facing, stitch up sides and continue down lining. Press seams open.
- Zigzag or overcast the bottom edge to finish.
- Sew on snap fasteners at the back.

Muff

This accessory kept delicate little hands warm on frosty cold days and was a handy place to keep a hanky.

Cutting list: Cut a rectangle 21.5cm (8½in) by 14cm (5½in) from fur and lining fabrics. (Before cutting out fur see page 9.)

Making up
- Trim 6mm (¼in) all around the fur rectangle.
- With right sides facing, pin the lining to the fur down the long sides. Place the pins at right angles, tucking the fur inside. Stitch together and turn.
- With right sides facing, fold the fur ends together and stitch closed. Take care not to catch the lining.
- Turn the lining edges in and whipstitch in place.
- Comb out any fur caught in the seams.

Adapt the Pattern

Haute couture is dramatically transformed into 'on safari' with a few simple changes. Make the outfit from khaki broadcloth. Shorten the sleeves and skirt, eliminate the fur collar, add box pleat pockets, buttons down the front and a belt.

The doll featured is an Elise doll originally sculpted by Jane Zidjunas. She stands 61cm (24in) high. If your doll does not have a bust, omit the bust darts from the pattern (see page 7).

Instructions for making T-strap slippers can be found in the Accessories section, page 80.

to complete the look •

Egyptian Chemise

'Turned up nose, turned down hose,
Flapper, yes sir, one of those,
Has anybody seen my gal?'

The discovery of Tutankhamun's tomb in 1922 brought a wave of romanticism known as Tutmania to the fashion conscious public. The stylized lines of Egyptian motifs were incorporated into the ever-popular art nouveau designs of the time. The loose shape of the chemise freed women from their corsets as the suffragette movement freed women in their thinking. Hair was bobbed, skirts were shortened and the Charleston and foxtrot became all the rage.

This outfit was designed for a 58-63.5cm (23-25in) doll.

you will need

½ metre/yard raw silk or rayon in main colour

¼ metre/yard same in second colour

Remnants of same in two other colours

Lightweight Vilene

2 metre/yard contrasting braid

Black beads

Fabric glue

5 snap fasteners

Chemise

Lapis lazuli, carnelian and gold on a background of Nile green are the colours used in this simple square-necked dress with three-quarter length sleeves and daring hemline. The lotus flower motif on the plastron and each end of a wide sash is outlined in black braid and trimmed with jet beads. The sleeves and part of the bodice are lined.

Pattern pieces required: Chemise front 1G, Chemise back 1H, Chemise sleeve 2J and Plastron 1I.

Cutting list: From the main colour cut one 1G, two 1H, four 2J and one lining hem panel 5cm (2in) deep by 40.5cm (16in) long. Cut one 1G and one 1H at indication marks for bodice lining. From second colour cut one 1I. From third colour cut a sash 91.5cm (36in) long by 5cm (2in) wide.

Making up

- Stitch darts in front starting at the widest part and running stitches off the tip of the dart and knotting the threads. Press darts down.
- With right sides facing, stitch front and backs at shoulders. Press seams open.
- Set in sleeves using Method 2 (see page 14). With right sides facing stitch up the sleeves and down the sides. Press seams open.
- Repeat these steps for the lining. Finish the bottom edge with a zigzag or overcast stitch.
- Work lotus motif on plastron (see box page 52).
- Using a short zigzag stitch, attach the plastron to the front of the

chemise at the neckline.

- Starting at the top, hand stitch braid trim around the plastron. Do not cut the ends off too short as they need to be caught in the seam when you stitch the lining on.
- With right sides facing, stitch lining to bodice around neckline and down the backs. Trim, turn and press seams open.
- With the sleeve linings inside the sleeves, overcast the end edges together. Turn up 6mm (¼in) and hem by hand. Hand stitch braid trim to sleeve about 6mm (¼in) from the edge. Snip open one or two stitches on the seam, tuck in the ends of the trim and stitch closed.
- Work decorative hem panel (see box page 53).
- With right sides facing, stitch decorative hem panel to hemline. Press seam down. With right sides facing, stitch lining hem panel to bottom of decorative hem panel and press seam up.
- Hand stitch braid trim to top and bottom of decorative hem panel.
- With right sides facing, stitch up

the back to indication mark. Make sure your decorative hem panel lines up when you stitch. Press seam open.

- Turn lining hem panel up and over decorative trim leaving 6mm (¼in) showing below the braid trim. Hand hem and press.
- Add braid trim around the neckline tucking in the ends around the edge.
- Add three snap fasteners at the back.

Sash

Make the sash from the third colour and stitch lotus motifs at each end. It ties around the hips over the chemise.

Making up

- With right sides together, fold sash lengthwise and stitch along long side. Turn to right side and press so seam runs down the centre.
- Glue lotus motifs A, B, C and E to the front ends with the curved edge of C overlapping the edge. Stitch braid trim around the edge, turning the ends of the braid under and add beads.
- Glue lotus motif C only, to the back of the sash/front motif. This encloses the raw edges of the sash.

Choker

The colours of the Egyptian choker match the colours of the decorative hem panel. The black lining folds over the front to form a border and it fastens with two small snap fasteners. The length and width depends on the size of the doll you are dressing.

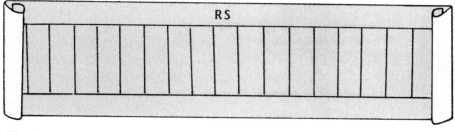

Fig 1

Making up

- Cut 3.5cm (1½in) lengths of different coloured fabrics in 2.5cm (1in) widths and stitch the pieces as for the hem panel. Press seams open, trimming if necessary.
- Iron interfacing to the back of the choker keeping the seams open. Check the choker length on the doll and adjust if necessary.
- Cut a lining 2.5cm (1in) wider and longer than the finished choker.
- With wrong sides facing, centre the choker on the lining and topstitch all around to hold in place, fold the edges of the lining over the choker, finishing with the ends, turning in the raw edges and creating a border, Fig 1. Hand stitch in place.
- Sew two snap fasteners at the back.

Lotus motif on plastron

Cutting list: Cut one C and three E in terracotta, one B in blue, one A in green, two D in blue and two D in green.

- Hand stitch flower stems in braid as shown on to plastron. Turn the ends under the plastron and tack in place.
- Iron interfacing to back of fabrics before cutting out lotus flower pieces.
- Glue motif C to the plastron covering the top of the braid stem. Glue motif B over C and motif A over B. Finally, glue E over end of A. Completed lotus flower Fig 2.
- Hand stitch braid trim around motif A first and then around complete motif. Add jet beads.
- Glue smaller motifs over ends of braid stems, overlapping the D's with E over the top.

Lotus flower pieces

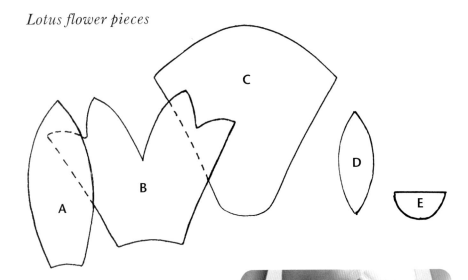

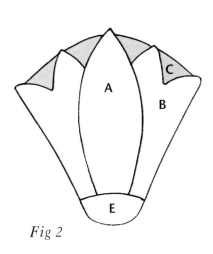

Fig 2

Instructions for making French knickers and long stockings can be found in the Underclothes section, page 66.

What's underneath?

Adapt the Pattern

Change the look of the chemise by flaring out the skirt from just below the arms and eliminating the sleeves. Change the shape of the plastron and add beads. Make the sash wider and tie it around the hips, blousing up the bodice.

Decorative hem

- Cut 5cm (2in) lengths of all four colours of fabric in widths varying from 12cm (½in) to 2.5cm (1in). Cut enough to go around the bottom of the chemise plus seam allowance.
- Stitch the pieces together widthways creating a banded pattern. Stitch two panels at a time, trim and press, and then stitch the pair to another pair and so on. When you have completed the band give it a final steam press on the front.

Baby Take a Bow

'Sugar and spice and all things nice, that's what little girl's are made of'

Lace, lace and yet more lace, what could be prettier than the lovely dress worn by Shirley Temple in the film *Stand Up and Cheer*. It is perfect for a party or a very special occasion.

This outfit fits a 43-48cm (17-19in) doll.

you will need

¼ metre/yard satin fabric

4 metre/4½ yard Chantilly lace, 4cm (1½in) wide

2 buttons

As many silk rosebuds as you like

The doll shown is a reproduction Shirley Temple doll M1106. She is 43cm (17in) high.

Instructions for making Mary Jane shoes can be found in the Accessories section, page 80.

to complete the look

Instructions

Dress

The dress is made from pale pink satin covered in Chantilly lace with a sash of delicate pink rosebuds. It has a high waist, low scoop neckline and buttons down the back. There are six rows of lace around the skirt and two rows of lace make up the sleeves.

Pattern pieces required: Party dress bodice front 2R, Party dress bodice back 2S, Party dress skirt front 2T and Party dress skirt back 2U.

Cutting list: From satin cut two 2R, four 2S (two reversed), one 2T and two 2U (one reversed).

Making up

- With right sides facing, stitch bodice front and backs together at shoulders. Press seams open. Repeat for lining.
- With right sides facing, stitch bodice and lining together around neck and down centre backs. Trim, turn and press.
- Zigzag stitch or overcast bodice and lining together at all raw edges. Bodice and lining are now worked as one unit.
- Stitch lace around armholes. Fold right sides together and stitch across lace ends and down side.

Instructions for making panties and ankle socks can be found in the Underclothes section, page 66.

- Stitch front and back skirts together at sides. Press seams open. Zigzag stitch or overcast top edge. Turn a 12mm (½in) hem at the bottom edge and hand stitch in place.
- Starting at the top of the skirt, topstitch six rows of lace on to the skirt to cover it.
- With right sides facing stitch skirt together at the back from indication mark to hem. Press seam open and stay stitch around opening.
- Gather the top edge of skirt and, with right sides together, stitch to bodice evening out the gathers. Press seam up.
- Make buttonholes in bodice and sew on buttons to match.
- Sew rosebuds across bodice as shown.

Adapt the Pattern

Change the party dress to a day dress by leaving the lace off and adding short or puffed sleeves. Add edging trim around the neck and sleeves and three decorative buttons down the front.

The doll shown is Twirp M1099, a French reproduction doll SFBJ 247 c.1915. He stands 56cm (22in) high.

Bib Overalls and Shirt

'Frogs and snails and puppy dog tails, that's what little boys are made of'

H uck Finn wore them fishing and Tom Sawyer wore them when painting a picket fence. Bib overalls were the standard dungarees for country boys working on the farm as well as city boys playing marbles.

This outfit fits a 51-56cm (20-22in) doll.

to complete the look •

Instructions for making a beanie and sandals can be found in the Accessories section, pages 74 and 80.

you will need

⅓ metre/yard denim or broadcloth

¼ metre/yard calico

6 buttons

1 set mini overall fasteners

Lightweight Vilene

Note: contrasting thread is optional for topstitching.

Overalls

The overalls pull up the body. The straps cross at the back and fasten to a front bib with overall fasteners. There are patch pockets on the bib and back, and set in pockets at the front. Contrast topstitching is applied.

Pattern pieces required: Overall front 4D, Overall back 4E, Bib 4F, Overall inner pocket 4B, Overall inner pocket lining 4C, Overall pocket 4G.

Cutting list: From denim/broadcloth cut two 4D (one reversed), two 4E (one reversed), two 4F, two 4B (one reversed), two 4C (one reversed), three 4G and two straps 4cm (1¾in) by 25.5cm (10in).

Making up

- Stitch down 6mm (¼in) at the top of the patch pocket. With right sides facing turn the top of the pocket over 12mm (½in) and stitch together at sides. Clip corners and turn to right side. Topstitch across the pocket to hold the turned edge in place. Turn the remaining edges in 6mm (¼in) and press. Complete two more pockets and pin one to bib and two to the back where indicated and topstitch in place.
- With right sides facing, stitch front overalls from crotch to top. Trim, turn and press. Repeat for back overalls.
- Stitch inner pocket lining to front, matching notches. Trim, turn, press and topstitch close to the edge.
- With right sides facing, stitch the inner pocket to the inner pocket

lining matching notches.
- With right sides facing, stitch front overalls to back overalls at the sides and inside legs. Press side seams towards the back and topstitch.
- With right sides facing, stitch bib front and back together leaving bottom edge open. Trim, turn, press and topstitch around sewn edge.
- Fold straps lengthwise, right sides facing and stitch long edge and across one end. Turn to right side and press.
- Zigzag or overcast waist edge of overalls, turn down 12mm (½in), pin bib inside centre front and straps inside back with raw edge matching notches and secure by topstitching two parallel rows around waist edge.
- Zigzag or overcast leg ends and turn under 3.5cm (1½in). Hand hem and topstitch edge. Turn up 2.5cm (1in) to form a cuff.
- Attach mini overall fasteners to the straps and sew the matching buttons on bib.

Shirt

The shirt buttons down the front, has long sleeves with buttoned cuffs and a pointed collar. The collar, cuffs and facings are faced with lightweight interfacing. Work run and fell seams at the shoulders, sleeve seams and sides (see page 11).

Pattern pieces required: Straight shirt front 5H, Straight shirt back 5I, Fitted shirt sleeve 2N, Pointed collar 1V and Straight shirt neck facing 5J.

Cutting list: From calico cut two 5H (one reversed), one 5I, two 2N, one 1V, one 5J and two cuffs 5cm (2in) by doll's wrist measurement plus 2.5cm (1in).

Making up
- With right sides facing, stitch fronts and back together at the shoulders.
- Work and attach shirt collar to neckline (see page 14).
- Stitch neck facing to ends of front facing. Press seams open and turn in 6mm (¼in) all around the outside edge of facing. Press.
- With right sides facing turn facing over and with collar sandwiched between facing and shirt, stitch around neck. Trim, turn and press.
- Work and set sleeves using Method 2 (see page 14).
- Make a bound opening in the sleeve end where indicated and set in cuff (see pages 14 and 15).
- Stitch a 6mm (¼in) hem around the bottom of the shirt.
- Work four buttonholes down the front and one at each of the cuffs and sew on buttons to match.

Instructions for making undershirt and underpants can be found in the Underclothes section, page 66.

what's underneath?

Adapt the Pattern
The overalls can be adapted in several ways. For summer make them into shorts, with or without pockets. Keep the bib and straps or use just straps. Eliminate the straps altogether and add an elasticized waistband. Make the shirt with short sleeves and add a pocket if you wish.

Prom Queen

'The most beautiful girl

in the world...'

Exams are over, school is out and the big night of celebration has come. A time to cherish and a time to remember with best friends, girl talk and the last dance of the evening with that special boy.

This outfit is designed to fit a 43-48cm (17-19in) doll.

you will need

½ metre/yard cotton batiste

1 metre/yard chiffon

Narrow bias binding matching cotton batiste

Narrow satin ribbon

60cm (24in) of satin ribbon
2.5cm (1in) wide

3 buttons

The doll shown is a Dianna Effner portrait head #1 design. She is 48cm (19in) high.

Instructions for making French slippers with trim can be found in the Accessories section, page 80.

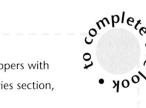

Instructions

Dress

This off-the-shoulder gown in flower print chiffon flowing over a skirt of soft blue cotton, has full puffed sleeves. For a romantic look there is a ruffle around the bodice and hem, which is accented by a narrow ribbon trim. A wide satin ribbon ties around the waist in a bow. The bodice is chiffon backed with cotton and lined with cotton to give it body; the sleeves and

Instructions for making French knickers can be found in the Underclothes section, see page 66. Make a half-petticoat as the dirndl skirt with two tiers of ruffles.

what's underneath?

ruffles are not. The cotton skirt and chiffon overskirt are worked separately and sewn to the bodice as one.

Pattern pieces required: Prom bodice front 1C, Prom bodice back 1D and Prom sleeve 1Y.

Cutting list: From cotton cut two 1C, four 1D (two reversed), and dirndl skirt four times the width of doll's waist measurement by approximately 23cm (9in) long. From chiffon cut one 1C, two 1D (one reversed), dirndl skirt the same dimensions as the cotton skirt, one neck ruffle 91.5cm (36in) long by 9cm (3½in) wide and one skirt ruffle

the same depth as the neck ruffle and twice the width of the skirt.

Making up

- Finish one edge of the neck and skirt ruffles by running a tiny, tight zigzag stitch or turning up a 3mm (⅛in) hem.
- Baste wrong side of chiffon bodices to right side of one set of cotton bodices. This will now work as a unit.
- Stitch chiffon bodice front and backs together at sides and press seams open. Repeat for lining.
- Backstitch darts in the backs starting at the widest part and running the stitch off the tip of the dart and knotting the threads. Press darts towards the centre. Repeat for lining.
- With right sides facing, stitch bodice to lining down back openings. Turn to right side and press. Stitch all three layers together at top front, around armholes and top of backs. Stitch just the chiffon and bodice facing (not the lining) at the bottom edge.
- Stitch sleeve together using a run and fell seam (see page 11). Run gathering stitches at the top of the sleeve. Stitch the bottom of sleeve to the bodice and pull the gathering stitches up to approximately 7.5cm (3in) at the top. Fig 1. Repeat for the other sleeve.
- Turn in short ends of neck ruffle and hand stitch in place. Press. Gather top edge of ruffle, adjusting the gathers evenly and, starting at back opening, pin around neckline and tops of sleeves. Stitch in place.
- Fold bias binding over the raw

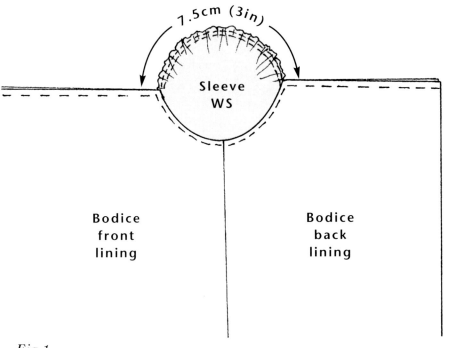

7.5cm (3in)

Sleeve
WS

Bodice
front
lining

Bodice
back
lining

Fig 1

Adapt the Pattern

This dress can be changed in many ways. Eliminate the sleeve, add the bodice ruffle at the sleeve line only or add decorative straps and silk flowers. A change of fabric alone gives an entirely different effect. Try satin, cotton, velvet, broderie anglaise or dotted Swiss voile.

edges and topstitch in place.

- Set shirring elastic 2.5cm (1in) above the edge of the sleeves (see page 11).
- Stitch the cotton skirt lining together from bottom to 5cm (2in) from the top. Press seam open.
- Stitch the chiffon skirt together from bottom to 5cm (2in) from the top using a run and fell seam.
- Stitch the skirt ruffle together across the short ends using a run and fell seam. Gather the top edge of the ruffle. With right sides facing, the seamed edge of the ruffle at the back of the skirt and matching raw edges, pin around the bottom of the chiffon skirt, distributing the gathers evenly. Stitch in place. Press the seam allowance up and stitch satin ribbon over the seam line making sure the raw edges are facing upwards.

- With chiffon skirt over skirt lining, working as one unit, run gathering stitches across the top of both. Pin to the bodice only, making sure the bodice lining is out of the way. Stitch in place. Trim, pull out the gathering stitches and press the seam allowance up into the bodice. Turn up the edge of the bodice lining and hand stitch over the skirt.
- Turn up 6mm (¼in) at the bottom of the skirt lining. Then turn up a hem so the lining ends at the top of the ruffle. Hand hem and press.
- Work buttonholes on bodice where indicated and sew on buttons to match. The neck ruffle covers the buttons.
- Tie satin ribbon around the waist in a bow at the back.

Circular Skirt and Blouse

*'One, two, three o'clock,
four o'clock rock!'*

Poodle skirts, net petticoats, bobby socks and saddle shoes! It's the fifties, school's out and it's down to the local malt or coffee shop. Drop a coin in the jukebox and get ready to rock and roll.

This outfit fits a 35.5-40.5cm (14-16in) doll.

The doll shown is an original Sweet Sue, an American Character Doll. She is 35.5cm (14in) high.

you will need

Square of wool felt large enough for the circumference of the skirt plus waistband

Small piece of contrasting felt

Two pompons

30cm (12in) of braid trim

Sequins, beads or rhinestones

Rickrack braid

Small amount of poplin in a small print, check or plaid

4 tiny buttons

1 hook and eye

Trim for collar

Lightweight Vilene

Instructions for making saddle shoes can be found in the Accessories section, page 80.

to complete the look

Skirt

The skirt is completely circular and lined with iron-on interfacing. It is decorated with a poodle dog motif.

Cutting list: The skirt is made from a circle of felt. The easiest way to find the correct size is to draw a circle the exact circumference of the doll's waist, in the centre of the felt. Measure the doll from waist to 12mm (1in) below the knee, then take that measurement from the edge of the drawn circle to mark the edge of the larger circle. Use a plate or circular tray to draw around. Iron on interfacing before cutting around outer and centre circle. From felt cut a waistband 3cm (1¼in) by doll's waist measurement plus 2.5cm (1in). From contrast felt cut poodle motif.

Making up

- Cut an opening from the waist circle just long enough for the skirt to slip over the doll's hips. Stay stitch around the opening to reinforce.

Instructions for making panties and bobby socks can be found in the Underclothes section, page 66. Make a half-petticoat from net as dirndl skirt with elasticized waist (see page 15).

What's underneath?

- Attach waistband to skirt, (see page 15). If making a small skirt, do this by hand and then topstitch using the machine.
- Glue the poodle motif in place. Hand stitch a length of fine cord or ribbon for a lead, tucking the end under the poodle's neck. Add sequins, beads or rhinestones to make a collar and make pompons (see page 78) to stitch on as shown.
- Stitch rickrack trim just above the edge of the skirt. It helps to hold the interfacing in place, as the skirt is not hemmed.
- Sew a hook and eye at the back of the waistband.

Blouse

The blouse has a round collar with inset trim, short sleeves and buttons down the front.

Pattern pieces required: Blouse front 4Z, Blouse back 5A, Blouse neck facing 5B, Round collar 1N and Short sleeve 2B.

Cutting list: Cut two 4Z (one reversed), one 5A, one 5B, two 1N and two 2B.

Making up

- With right sides facing, join fronts and back at shoulders. Press seams open.
- With right sides facing, stitch neck facing to ends of front facings. Press seams open and turn in 6mm (¼in) all around outside edge of facing. Press.
- Work collar with inset trim and attach to neck (see page 14).
- With right sides facing, turn facing over and with collar sandwiched between facing and blouse, stitch around neck. Trim, turn to right side and press.

- Turn up 3mm (⅛in) at end of sleeve. Set in sleeves using Method 2 (see page 14).
- Turn up a further 12mm (½in) at sleeve ends and hand hem.
- Stitch a 6mm (¼in) hem at the bottom of the blouse.
- Blind stitch facing to blouse front.
- Work buttonholes where indicated and sew on buttons to match.

Adapt the Pattern

Make the blouse with a back opening, Peter Pan collar and puffed sleeves with rickrack trim. The circular skirt made from cotton fabric will give the same fullness as the felt skirt, but with a softer drape. A ribbon tie with pompons on the ends keeps the fifties feel.

What's Underneath

*T*his section offers a variety of undergarments worn under the costumes that appear in this book. Like the clothes, the undergarments are not an authentic representation, rather a simplified version of the original. Traditional drawers, for example, buttoned at the back and were split except at the waistband. Most of the underclothing is made up in white fabric (with the exception of the red flannel petticoat), but pastel shades or trimmings can be lovely especially if they match the clothing.

Fabric suggestions:
Cotton batiste, poplin, lawn, calico, organza, silk, satin, broderie anglaise, flannel, winceyette and net.

Trimming suggestions:
Fine flat lace, ruffled lace, eyelet lace, small bows, ribbons and ribbon flowers.

Notions:
Buttons, snap fasteners, elastic, shirring elastic and bias tape.

Instructions for making the Teddy (left) can be found on page 73.

Instructions

Drawers

The drawers are straight-legged with an elasticized waistline and are made from poplin, cotton lawn, or broderie anglaise. Traditionally they were white and cotton drawers normally had pin tucks (see page 44), lace or ribbon at the bottom.

Pattern piece required: Drawers 4L.

Cutting list: Cut two 4L (one reversed). Place pattern on fold, cut around outside edge. Open out fabric and cut around inner edge on one half only.

Making up

- If you are making pintucks do it before positioning the pattern on the fabric and cutting out.
- With right sides together, stitch fronts and backs together at crotch. Clip curves and press seams open.
- Add lace or trim to bottom of legs (optional).
- Stitch up 6mm (¼in) from the bottom of leg then, with right sides facing pin each leg, matching the pintucks, lace and trim, and stitch up one leg and down the other. Press seam open.
- Make an elasticized casing for flat elastic at waist (see page 11).
- Turn up 6mm (¼in) at hemline and stitch in place.

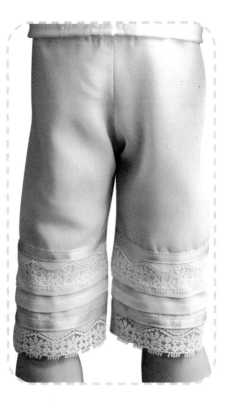

Bloomers

Bloomers are fuller than drawers and were sometimes worn under dresses and swimming costumes and made from the same fabric. The waist and legs are elasticized. Lightweight fabrics could have a ruffle at the gathered leg.

Pattern pieces required: Bloomers 4W.

Cutting list: Cut two 4W (one reversed). Place pattern on fold, cut around outside edge. Open out fabric and cut around inner edge on one half only.

Making up

- With right sides facing, stitch bloomers together at front and back. Notch and press seams open.
- Stitch together at crotch. Press seam open.
- Make an elasticized casing for flat elastic at waist and sew shirring elastic at legs (see page 11).

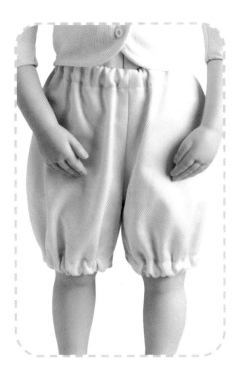

French knickers

French knickers are full fitting with an elasticized waistline and loose around the legs. They are usually in white with an optional lace trim.

Pattern pieces required: French knickers 4J.

Cutting list: Cut two 4J (one reversed).

Making up
- With right sides facing stitch fronts and backs together at crotch. Clip curves and press seams open.
- Turn a 6mm (¼in) hem at the legs. Add lace edging (optional).
- Set shirring elastic 12mm (½in) up from edge (see page 11).
- With right sides facing, pin each leg together and stitch across crotch.
- Make an elasticized casing for flat elastic at waist (see page 11).

Panties

Panties became popular in the 1940s. They were close fitting knickers made from cotton in white, pastels or tiny print fabric with elasticized waist and legs and optional lace trim.

Pattern pieces required: Small panties 4H or Large panties 4I.

Cutting list: Cut one 4H or 4I.

Making up
- Turn in 3mm (⅛in) around the leg openings and press in place. Clip into the pressed edge to ease, which allows you to turn in another 3mm (⅛in) without the fabric puckering. Stitch in place. It is easier to turn a tiny hem if you start pinning in the middle and work out.
- Press leg openings and attach trim.
- With right sides facing, stitch sides together.
- Make an elasticized casing for flat elastic at waist (see page 11).

Underpants

The boy's pants have an elasticized waist, loose leg openings and fly front. Make from winceyette – a child's undershirt (vest) is perfect for the fabric. Place the pattern with the leg edge at a hemline or sleeve end, to give a realistic edge.

Pattern pieces required: Underpants 4K.

Cutting list: Cut two 4K and two flies following the guideline.

Making up
- With right sides facing, stitch fronts and backs together at crotch. Clip curves and turn. Press.
- Make an elasticized casing for flat elastic at waist (see page 11).
- Stitch the two flies together leaving top open for turning. Trim and turn to right side, fold top edges in and press. Pin to front with straight side on the seam and topstitch in place around the fly.
- Sew two buttons on the fly.

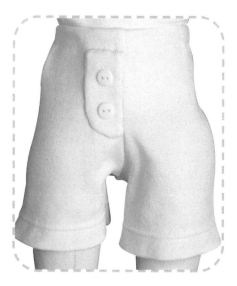

Camisole

This delicate garment is usually made from white or pastel-coloured silk or batiste. Decorated with white work, lace and ribbons, it fastens down the front and is fully lined.

Pattern pieces required: Camisole front 4M and Camisole back 4N.

Cutting list: Cut four 4M (two reversed) and two 4N.

Making up

- Add lace and ribbon trim to the bodice fronts.
- Stitch bodice fronts and bodice back together at shoulders. Press seams open. Repeat for lining.
- With right sides of bodice and lining facing, stitch around neck opening, down fronts and around armholes. Trim.
- With right sides of bodice and lining facing, stitch sides together. Press seams open, turn bodice over lining and press again.
- Turn a 6mm (¼in) hem along the bottom edge and topstitch in place. Press.
- Sew snap fasteners down the front and stitch optional ribbon bows over the snaps.

Liberty bodice

This sleeveless vest worn by children is made from winceyette or heavy cotton fabric and is fully lined with cotton or lawn. It buttons down the front and the edges are finished with bias binding.

Pattern pieces required: Liberty bodice front 4R and Liberty bodice back 4S.

Cutting list: Cut four 4R (two reversed) and two 4S.

Making up

- Stitch fronts and backs together at shoulders and down sides. Press seams open. Repeat for lining.
- With wrong sides together, baste the bodice and lining together around edges.
- Bind all edges with medium width bias tape and topstitch in place, turning in the ends.
- Work four buttonholes and stitch on buttons to match.

Petticoat

Dresses with full skirts always had a petticoat or two under them. They were made from white cotton lawn, poplin or batiste decorated with pin tucks, ruffles and lace. For a more luxurious feel make it from silk or taffeta. In Victorian times young girls always wore a petticoat of red flannel as the first layer.

Pattern pieces required: Petticoat bodice front 4P and Petticoat bodice back 4Q.

Cutting list: Cut two 4P, four 4Q and one skirt three to four times the doll's waist measurement by the desired length plus seam allowances and hem.

Making up
- With right sides facing, stitch bodice front to bodice backs at shoulders. Press seams open. Repeat for lining.
- With right sides of bodice and lining facing, stitch around neck opening, down the backs and around armholes. Trim.
- With right sides of bodice and lining facing, stitch sides together. Press seams open, turn bodice over lining and press again.
- Work skirt as dirndl and attach to bodice (see page 15).
- Work buttonhole closures where indicated.
- Trim hem edge (optional).

Half-petticoat

The half-petticoat is worked as a dirndl skirt with waistband (see page 15). Its length depends on the length of the skirt it is worn under. Several could be worn together and in the 1950s, layers of net were used for added fullness. A net petticoat is sewn directly on to a waistband made from elastic.

A-line petticoat

The A-line petticoat is made from the same pattern pieces as the overskirt of the outfit. Instead of a waistband sew a casing at the top and insert flat elastic (see page 11). Make up the petticoat following the instructions given in the pattern. Try the petticoat on the doll with the skirt to determine the length before hemming. A lace trim and tiny flower motifs add a decorative touch.

Undershirt (vest)

Make this boys' undergarment from winceyette or a child's undershirt (vest). Place the pattern pieces so that the neck and sleeve edges of the vest make authentic edgings.

Pattern pieces required: Undershirt front/back 4T and Undershirt sleeve 4U.

Cutting list: Cut two 4T and two 4U.

Making up
- With right sides facing, stitch shirt front and back together at shoulders.
- Set sleeves using Method 2 (see page 14).
- Overcast bottom edge, turn up 6mm (¼in) and run two rows of topstitching.
- Hem the sleeve ends in the same way as the bottom edge and bind the neck opening with a bias strip of self-fabric.

Socks and stockings

Make these from children's socks using the top edge as the top of the doll's socks. Cut the foot end of the sock off and cut the tube in half lengthwise so you have two pieces. Measure piece snugly around doll's leg and using a short stitch on your machine, stitch rounding off one corner. Fig 1. Trim close to the seam and turn right side out. Lace tights, stretch cotton, and T-shirts also make up well.

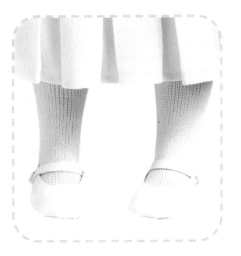

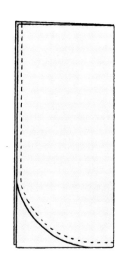

Fig 1

Combinations

Made from winceyette, flannel or cotton fabric, this one-piece undergarment was worn by girls and young children of both sexes. Add a lace trim for girls and leave untrimmed for boys. The bodice is lined in self-fabric.

Pattern pieces required: Combination pants 4V, Combination bodice front 4X and Combination bodice back 4Y.

Cutting list: Cut two 4V (one reversed), four 4X (two reversed) and two 4Y (one reversed).

Making up
- Stitch lace trim, if used, to the bodice fronts and pants where indicated.
- With right sides facing, stitch fronts and back together at shoulders. Press seams open. Repeat for lining.
- With right sides facing, stitch bodice and lining together around neck and arm openings. Trim, turn to right side and press.
- With right sides facing, stitch bodice and lining together at sides. Press seams open, turn lining over and press again.
- Gather pants at back where indicated. Stitch pants to lining at waistline. Press seam allowance towards lining.
- Zigzag stitch or overcast long edge of flap at front of pants. Fig 1. With right sides facing stitch pant backs together from crotch to top and pant fronts together from crotch to indication mark. Stitch several times at the indication mark to reinforce then snip seam allowance to the reinforcing stitches. Fig 2.
- With right sides facing, stitch bodice and lining together at front openings. Clip corners, turn and press. Hand stitch lining over seam allowance at waistline.
- With right sides facing, stitch legs together from crotch. Turn up and stitch a 6mm (¼in) hem and, if used, add a row of lace.
- Work three buttonholes and sew on buttons to match.

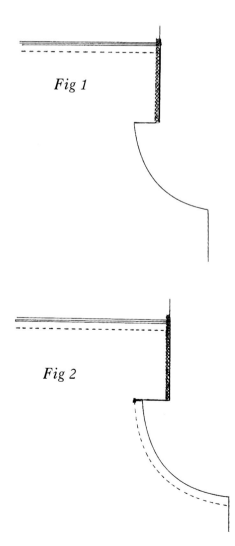

Fig 1

Fig 2

Teddy

This variation of the combination is made from silk or satin. The self-lined bodice has two rows of elasticized casings.

Pattern pieces required Teddy front/back 2F.

Cutting list Cut two 2F, two linings 8cm (3⅛in) wide by 56cm (22½in) deep and two pieces of 12mm (½in) wide ribbom 16cm (6½in) long in matching colour.

Making up
- With right sides facing, stitch from top to crotch on both sides of Teddy. Trim and finish seams with a zigzag stitch.
- Stitch lining together at short ends.
- Stitch lace trim to the ribbon straps and with right sides facing, pin them where indicated. Try Teddy on doll and adjust straps.
- With right sides facing, stitch lining to Teddy at top, at the same time incorporating the ribbon straps. Turn to right side and press flat.

- Stitch lace trim across top of Teddy.
- Turn up 6mm (¼in) at bottom of lining and set elastic at the top and bottom using lining as casing. Be sure you measure your doll at the points where the elastic will go. Don't make it too tight.
- Turn up a tiny hem at legs and stitch on lace trim. With right sides facing, stitch up one leg and down the other. Trim and finish seam with a zigzag.
- Add two small bows at bodice.

Hats

*I*n the past almost every outfit had a matching hat in an instantly recognizable style. These hats are simple to make and trimmed with feathers, beads or a pompon they add the perfect finishing touch.

Instructions

Beanie

This hat is made from six segments of calico, alternating blue and red, and lined with blue calico. You could make each segment of the crown a different colour or the same colour. The crown and peak are interfaced but it can be made without the peak. The propeller is optional and could be replaced with a pompon or covered button.

you will need

Small amounts of calico in different colours

Medium weight iron-on interfacing

Small piece of yellow card

Pattern pieces required: Beanie peak 5R and Beanie crown 5S.

Cutting list: From blue calico cut nine 5S and two 5R. From red calico cut three 5S.

Making up
• Follow instructions for the peak cap.
• Cut propeller from yellow card. If the card is thin, use two pieces and glue them together. Stick a glass-headed pin through the centre of the propeller pushing it to the top. Stick the pin in the top of the cap and push a tiny bead on the point and glue to secure.

Peak cap

The cap is made from worsted wool to match the Norfolk suit, but it could also be made from velvet, corduroy, cotton broadcloth or tweed. It is fully lined with cotton fabric and the peak is stiffened with buckram. The cap and the lining are worked separately.

you will need

⅛ metre/yard worsted wool

⅛ metre/yard cotton or satin lining fabric

1 shank button (cover in self-fabric or use a leather one)

Small amount of buckram

Pattern pieces required: Peak cap peak 5K and Peak cap crown 5L.

Cutting list: From wool cut two 5K and six 5L. From lining cut six 5L.

Making up

- Working on two sections of the crown at a time, match the notches and stitch one side from the bottom to the top, making three units of two sections.
- Stitch two of the units together in the same way and continue until all six sections are sewn together. Press the seams open. Repeat these steps for the lining and set aside.
- With right sides of the peak together add buckram to one side, pin and stitch around the outer edge of the cap.
- With right sides facing, pin the peak to the cap. To make cap stand up, centre the peak on a seam. For a flatter look, centre over a section. Stitch in place.
- Cover button and attach to the top of the cap where all the seams meet.
- With right sides of cap and lining together, stitch around the edge of the cap leaving a small opening at the back for turning. Trim around the edge, except for the opening, and turn the cap through the lining. Slipstitch the opening together and steam press the edges so that the lining stays up inside the cap.

Glengarry bonnet

A traditional Glengarry bonnet is made from tartan fabric with a feather pinned to the side but this basic hat pattern can become a dozen other styles including the pillbox. To match the coat, make the bonnet from the same mohair fabric.

you will need

A small amount of mohair or fur fabric

The same amount of fabric in cotton or satin

Pattern pieces required: Cloche crown 5N and Cloche side crown 5P.

Cutting list: From mohair cut one 5N and one 5P. From lining cut one 5N and one 5P.

Making up

- With right sides facing, stitch the side crown together at the sides. Repeat for lining.
- Stitch the crown to the side crown. Repeat for lining.
- With right sides facing, stitch the side crown and side crown lining together around the bottom edge leaving 5cm (2in) open at the back for turning.
- Turn bonnet to right side, turn raw edges in at opening and hand stitch closed.
- Comb out any fur trapped in the seams.

Merry Widow hat

Made from black velvet, it is interlined with buckram to enable the brim to be turned up. The crown is lined with satin and topped with an aigrette of raven black feathers.

you will need

¼ metre/yard of velvet

¼ metre/yard of buckram

Small amount of satin or cotton lining fabric

An aigrette of feathers

Pattern pieces required: Merry Widow brim 5T, Merry Widow crown 5V, Merry Widow side crown 5U.

Cutting list: From velvet cut two 5T, one 5V and one 5U. From lining cut one 5V and one 5U. From buckram cut one each of 5T, 5V and 5U

Note: Lay the velvet face side down on a Turkish towel when you are steam pressing.

Making up

- With right sides facing, stitch side seams of all velvet and lining brims and side crowns. Press seams open.
- Overlap buckram brim at side and tack together. Do the same with the buckram side crown.
- With right sides facing, with buckram on top, stitch brims together around the outside. Trim the buckram close to the seam and turn the brim to the right side. Press.
- Stitch crown to side crown matching notches. Repeat for the buckram. Repeat for the lining. Trim.
- Push the buckram crown up inside the crown to match inside crown and stitch in place around the edge.
- Stitch the brim to the crown matching notches. Trim.
- Push the lining up into the crown with right side showing, turn the edge under and hand stitch to the brim to finish.
- Turn the right side of the brim up at a fashionable angle and stitch the feathers behind the brim.

Mob cap

Simply made from a circle of cotton fabric, the cap is gathered all around by elastic, with a ruffle of eyelet lace trimming the edge.

you will need

¼ metre/yard cotton batiste or poplin

Gathered eyelet lace (measurement taken from circumference of cap)

Narrow flat elastic

Narrow ribbon

Cutting list: Draw a circle using the following dimensions. If you do not have a compass, a plate or a round serving tray makes a good template.

Fig 1

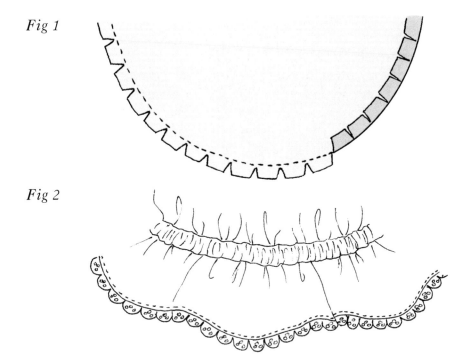

Fig 2

35.6-40.6cm (4-16in) doll: 20.4cm (8in) diameter.

43.2-48.2cm (17-19in) doll: 25.4cm (10in) diameter.

50.8-55.9cm (20-22in) doll: 30.5cm (12in) diameter.

58.4-63.5cm (23-25in) doll: 33 cm (13in) diameter.

Making up

- Stay stitch 6mm (¼in) in from edge. Notch up to the stitching being careful not to cut into it. Fig 1.
- Turn up the edge following the line of stitching and press in place.
- Pin eyelet trim underneath the edge and topstitch in place. Hand stitch ribbon trim to the underside of the cap, covering the line of stitching.
- Using a pencil, lightly draw a line 3cm (1¼in) in from the outside edge. Measure shirring elastic around the doll's head – not too tight, but not too loose, and mark the elastic. Cut the elastic off several inches from the mark to let

you pull the elastic up to the mark while you are stitching.

- Secure the end of the elastic to a point on the pencil line and using the line as a guide, attach the elastic to the cap pulling up as you sew. When you reach the end of the line, secure the elastic at the indication mark and cut remaining end off. Fig 2.

Motoring bonnet

The bonnet is made from a purchased straw hat painted with fabric paint. Choose a colour which will hide the road dust when motoring. A veil is secured at the top of the bonnet and fastens under the chin.

you will need

Straw hat (purchased from craft or doll shop)

½ metre/yard chiffon fabric by 92cm (36in) long

Making up

- About 2.5cm (1in) from the edge of the rectangle, run a narrow tight zigzag stitch all around. Do not try to run the stitch at the very edge, as this is extremely difficult to do. If your machine does not have a zigzag stitch, run two or three lines of stitching as close together as you can get them, so that the fabric does not show between the stitching but appears as one row. Carefully trim the excess fabric as close to the stitching as you can without cutting into it.
- Run a gathering stitch down the centre width of the veil. Pull stitches up to fit over the crown of the hat and secure.
- Fasten veil across the brim with a few hand stitches.

Sailor hat

The hat is made from two circles of fabric, a band decorated with two parallel rows of decorative braid and a pompon on the top. The hat can be turned into a beret by eliminating the band and pompon and binding the opening,

you will need

Fabric to match the sailor outfit

66cm (26in) soutache braid

1 pompon (see box)

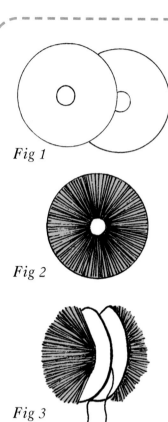

Fig 1

Fig 2

Fig 3

Pompon

The size of the pompon determines the size you cut the template. Cut two template circles from stiff cardboard with a 12mm (½in) diameter hole in the centre of each. Fig 1. Place the templates together and wind yarn through the centre hole and around the outside closely and evenly keeping it taut but not tight. Continue until the template is covered. Fig 2. Snip through the yarn at the outside edge between the templates with sharp scissors. Ease a piece of yarn between the two templates, wind around several times and tie firmly. Fig 3. Remove the templates and trim the pompon if needed. It is now ready to sew to the top of a hat. Ready-made pompons can be bought in various sizes.

Pattern pieces required: Sailor hat crown/brim 5Q.

Cutting list: Before cutting check the measurement of your doll's head and make any adjustments. Cut two 5Q. From one of the circles cut out centre where indicated.
Cut one band 33cm (13in) long by 5.5cm (2¼in) wide.
Note: Zigzag stitching or overcasting edges of the band eliminates bulk when working with heavier fabrics. If you make the hat from a lightweight fabric like cotton, turn the edge of the band in rather than overcasting before stitching in place.

Making up
• With wrong sides facing, fold the band in half, lengthwise and press. Open it out and topstitch two rows of soutache braid to one side of the fold. Stitch the first row close to the fold and the second row 6mm (¼in) from the first row leaving about 12mm (½in) to the raw edge.
• Stitch the band together at the short ends.
• With right sides facing, stitch top of band to the underside of the crown opening. Trim and clip seam allowance.
• With band facing up, topstitch the seam allowance towards the band.
• Zigzag or overcast the other edge of the band; turn it up over the seam allowance and hand stitch in place.
• With right sides facing match top crown to under crown and stitch together around edge. Turn to right side and press.
• Stitch pompon to centre top of hat.

Wide brim cloche

The cloche is a versatile style that can be made up in various fabrics and simply or elaborately decorated. It is interfaced and the crown lined with satin.

you will need

¼ metre/yard velvet

¼ metre/yard medium weight Vilene

Small amount of satin lining fabric

1 metre/yard double-sided satin ribbon

Small amount of windowpane net

An aigrette of feathers

Pattern pieces required: Cloche brim 5M, Cloche crown 5N, Cloche side crown 5P.

Cutting list: Before cutting out, iron medium weight interfacing to the wrong side of the velvet fabric with velvet side face down on a Turkish towel. Transfer the pattern markings to interfaced side. From velvet cut two 5M (one reversed), one 5N and one 5P. From satin cut one 5N and one 5P.

Making up

- Stitch together back of each brim piece and side crown. Trim corners of seam allowance, turn and press seams open. Repeat for side crown of lining.
- With right sides together, stitch brim pieces together around outer edge. Notch and turn the brim right side out. Stitch the layers together at the inner edge. Press.
- Pin top crown to side crown and with top crown flat on machine plate, stitch gently around, guiding the side crown edge in line with the curve. Trim and turn the crown right side out. Repeat for lining.
- Stitch the brim and side crown together from the inside of the crown. Clip into the seam allowance around the edge within 2mm (¹⁄₁₆in) of the seam line. Make clips at 12mm (½in) intervals around the circumference.
- Run a guideline stitch around and 12mm (½in) up from the edge of the lining. Notch as for hat and turn the notched edge up just above the guideline, with wrong sides facing, and press.
- Push the lining up into the hat, wrong sides facing and matching the back seams, and hand stitch to the side crown.
- Wrap satin ribbon around the base of the crown and tack in place at the front of the hat. Make a bow and tack to the front covering the hatband stitches.
- Tack windowpane net around the front and sides and add feathers.

Shoes and Boots

*I*f you are able to create the clothes in this book there is no reason why you cannot create the perfect shoe to go with the outfit. Making shoes is not difficult; it just requires time, patience and a little extra effort. Shoes, like hats add a degree of authenticity to the outfit and give you an area in which to experiment with your creativity. A delicate slipper of the same fabric as a party dress will make the outfit come together.

Shoes and boots overlapped the periods in which they were worn and only a few definite styles can be pinned down to a precise period of time with certain styles returning in fashion over the years. Shoes and boots can be made from pliable leather, glove leather, imitation leather (Rexine) and suede. Shoes and slippers can also be made from fabrics like pinwale corduroy, canvas, brocade and satin.

you will need

Leather or fabric

Heavyweight iron-on interfacing for fabrics that need reinforcing

Cardboard. (The kind found on the back of writing pads is perfect. Anything heavier will be too thick. Cereal packages are too thin.)

Strong craft glue

Clothes pegs

Shoe dye for leather shoes

Crochet thread for laces

Shank or boot buttons

Scissors for cutting card

Craft knife

Awl

Trimmings

Tips • Tips • Tips • Tips • Tips •

- If you make a mistake when topstitching leather, it is best to cut a new piece rather than removing the stitching as the needle holes will remain, so work slowly and try to get your stitches even the first time.
- If using imitation leather, the back and the edges will be white. Paint shoe renovator or dye, the same colour as the leather, carefully around all the edges that will show when the shoe is finished.
- Tissue paper stuffed into the toe of the shoe will help stretch it to a nice rounded shape.

Instructions

General instructions

- If the fabric is quite flimsy or stretches like glove leather, back the whole shoe with interfacing before cutting out. If the shoes or boots have buttons and the leather does not need to be lined, iron interfacing where the buttons will go before cutting out the pattern piece. Do not press too hard and do not use steam, as the leather will stretch.
- Remember to reverse pieces as instructed when cutting out so you do not end up with two left feet.
- Slashes, shoelace holes and decorative holes are cut out before the shoe is stitched together.
- Cut two soles and two inner soles from cardboard. It can be turned to either side so it is not necessary to reverse them.

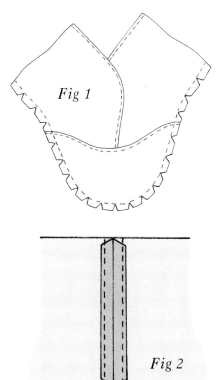

Fig 1

Fig 2

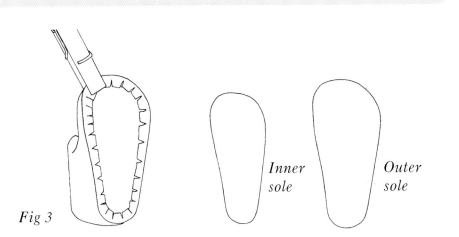

Fig 3

Inner sole *Outer sole*

- Remember to cut leather soles for one left and one right foot.
- Run a line of stay stitching 6mm (¼in) in around the lower edge of the uppers. Cut notches fairly close together in curved areas below the stay stitching. Fig 1.
- Stitch the back of the shoe together, open out the seam, clip the corners off the top and bottom, and stitch each side down. Fig 2. Trim off excess.
- Insert cardboard sole, glue around notched edge of shoe upper and press to sole. Use the stay stitching as a guideline. It should be just under the sole. Mould the edges smoothly and clamp all around with clothes pegs. Fig 3. Wipe off excess glue with a wet cloth. The glue should set quickly so don't leave the pegs on the shoe too long as they can mark the leather.
- When the sole has dried, spread glue on the inner cardboard sole and press in place filling the area inside the shoe. Use clothes pegs to hold it in place until dry.
- When the inner sole is fixed, spread glue over the bottom of the shoe and fix the leather sole. Make sure the edges are securely glued.

Mary Jane shoes

Pattern pieces required: Upper 6E, Sole 6F and Inner sole 6G.

Cutting list: From fabric cut two 6E, two 6F and two straps approximately 6mm (¼in) wide to fit over doll's foot plus 12mm (½in). From cardboard cut two 6F and two 6G.

Making up

- Stitch the straps inside the shoe upper where indicated.
- Round off the other ends of the straps and cut a slit for a small shank button or bead to fit through.
- Follow general instructions to make up shoe.
- Stitch the button/bead to the outside of shoe.

Sandals, Ankle or T-straps

Pattern pieces required: Sandal upper 6N, Shoe strap 6P, Sole 6F and Inner Sole 6G. (For ankle strap shoes use the Mary Jane upper 6E.)

Cutting list: From fabric cut two 6N, two 6P and two 6F. From cardboard cut two 6F and two 6G.

Making up

- Cut out pattern on upper for sandals. (If you are making T-strap or ankle shoes omit pattern.)
- Centre the back of the strap to the back seam of the upper. Make sure the long end of the strap comes from the inner edge of the shoe to feed through the tongue and fasten on the outer side. Glue to hold and topstitch in place.
- Follow general instructions.

Slippers

Pattern pieces required: Upper 6E, Sole 6F and Inner Sole 6G.

Cutting list: From fabric cut two 6E and two 6F. From cardboard cut two 6F and two 6G.

Making up

- Work in the same way as the Mary Jane's, eliminating the straps.
- Add decorative florets, buckles and bows to the toes.
- If you are making carpet slippers, make them from pinwale corduroy, felt, flannel or satin backed with interfacing and sew pompons on the toes.

Saddle shoes

The trim is made in black, navy or brown; the rest of the shoe is in white. Turn the shoe into an Oxford by making up in all one colour.

Pattern pieces required: Saddle shoe upper 6Q, Saddle shoe trim 6R, Saddle shoe sole 6S, Saddle shoe inner sole 6T and Saddle shoe tongue 6U.

Cutting list: From white fabric cut two 6Q, two 6R and two 6U. From trim colour cut two 6R. From cardboard cut two 6S and two 6T.

Making up

- Using an awl, make holes on trim where indicated.
- Glue the tongue under the upper, and the trim on top of the upper and topstitch in place using white thread to contrast on the colour.
- Follow general instructions.
- Insert crochet thread for ties.

Balmoral boots

The boots are made from leather and trimmed with narrow seam binding which could be a contrasting colour. They lace up the front with four eyelets on either side.

Pattern pieces required: Balmoral boot upper 5Z, Balmoral boot toe 6A, Balmoral boot sole 6B, Balmoral boot inner sole 6C and Balmoral boot tongue 6D.

Cutting list: From leather cut four 5Z (two reversed), two 6A, two 6B (one reversed), and two 6D. From cardboard cut two 6B and two 6C.

Making up

- Using an awl, make holes on each side of the uppers where indicated.

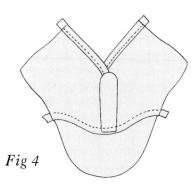

Fig 4

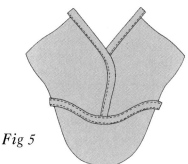

Fig 5

- Bind and stitch the top edge of the toes and the top edge of the uppers with seam binding. Leave about 6mm (¼in) overlapping all edges.
- Match and glue uppers at A to the centre of the toe. Glue tongue behind uppers at centre. Fig 4. Turn shoe over and topstitch in place. Fig 5.
- Stitch lower edge of boot and notch.

- Stitch back of boot together as in general instructions.
- Complete boots following the general instructions.
- Insert crochet thread into holes for ties.

High-buttoned boot

The boot has a scalloped boot flap with four boot buttons and is made from leather.

Pattern pieces required: High-buttoned boot outside upper 6H, High-buttoned boot inside upper 6I, High-buttoned boot toe 6J, High-buttoned boot flap 6K, High-buttoned boot sole 6L and High-buttoned boot inner sole 6M.

Cutting list: From leather cut two 6H (one reversed), two 6I (one reversed), two 6J, two 6K (one reversed) and two 6L (one reversed). From cardboard cut two 6L and two 6M.

Making up
- Cut buttonholes on flaps where indicated.
- Match flap to inside upper and with right sides together, stitch from A to B. Fig 6. Clip seam allowance at curve, across seam allowance corners and trim.
- Run a line of stay stitching close to the top of the uppers. Work in an assembly line method. Fig 7.
- Topstitch uppers at the top, down the front and around the scallops.
- Stitch outside upper to inside upper from C to D and open out seam.
- Glue and topstitch toe to uppers. Fig 8.
- Stitch backs together as in general instructions.
- Stitch lower edge of boot 6mm (¼in) up from edge and notch to stitching every 12mm (½in). Fig 9.
- Follow general instructions.
- Sew on boot buttons.

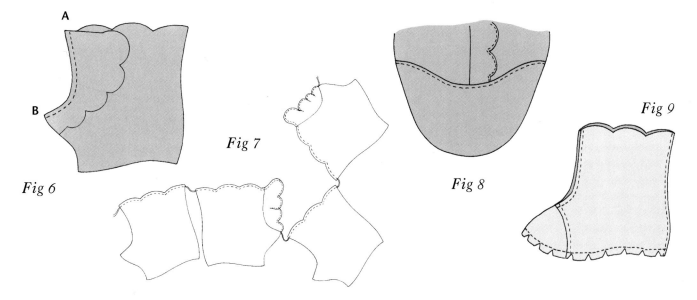

Fig 6

Fig 7

Fig 8

Fig 9

Pattern Index

Patterns

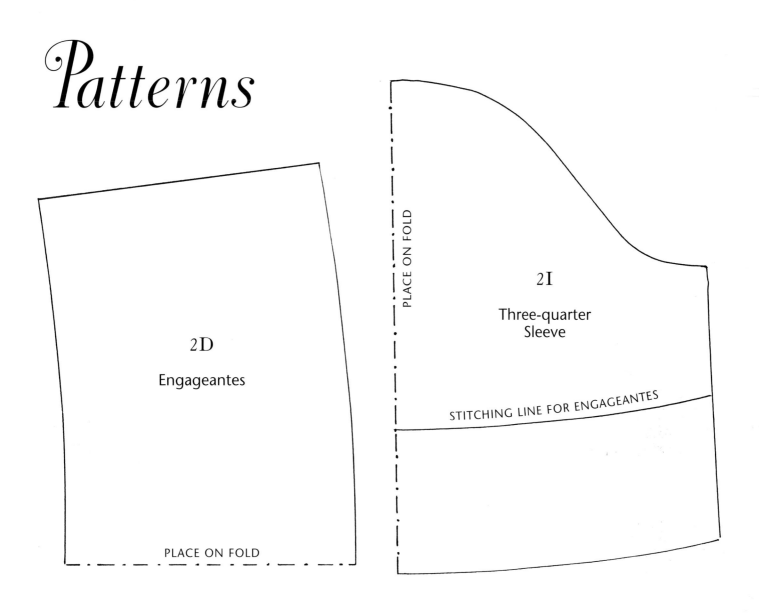

2D

Engageantes

PLACE ON FOLD

PLACE ON FOLD

2I

Three-quarter
Sleeve

STITCHING LINE FOR ENGAGEANTES

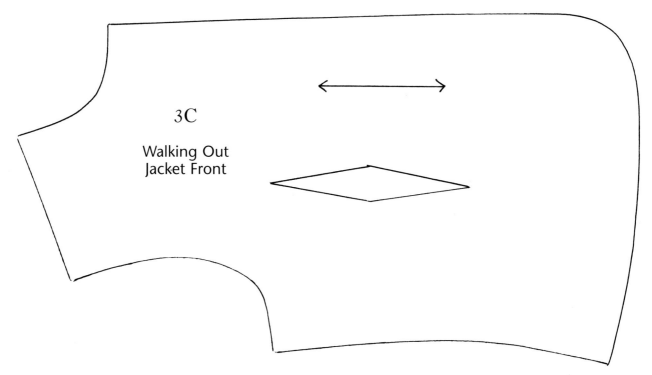

3C

Walking Out
Jacket Front

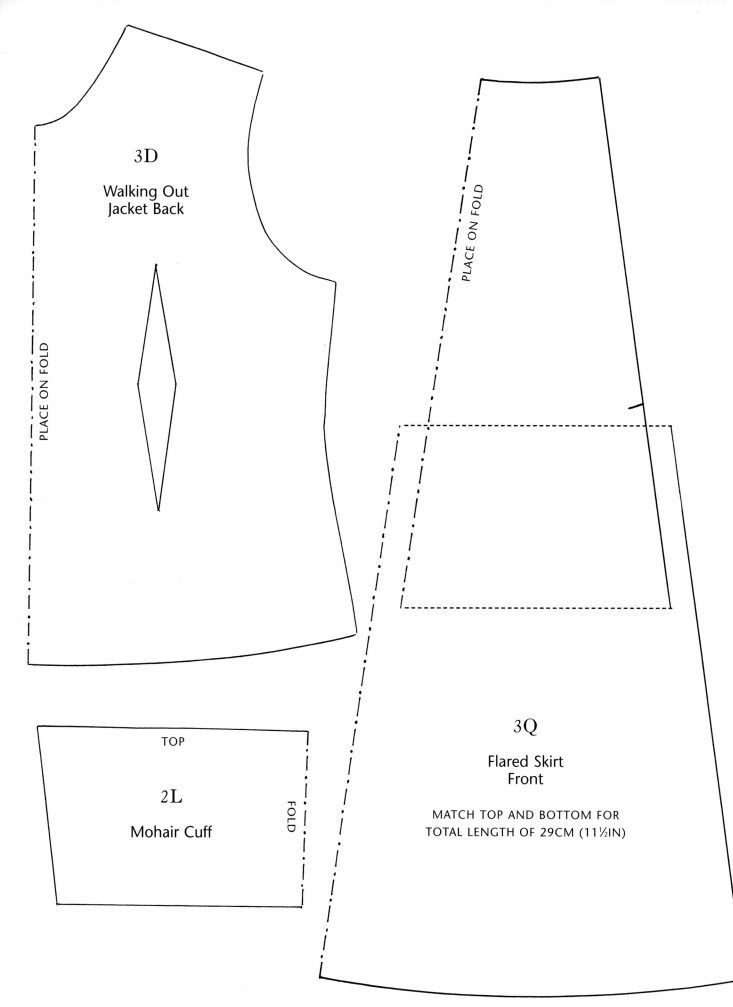

3D

Walking Out Jacket Back

PLACE ON FOLD

TOP

2L

Mohair Cuff

FOLD

PLACE ON FOLD

3Q

Flared Skirt Front

MATCH TOP AND BOTTOM FOR
TOTAL LENGTH OF 29CM (11½IN)

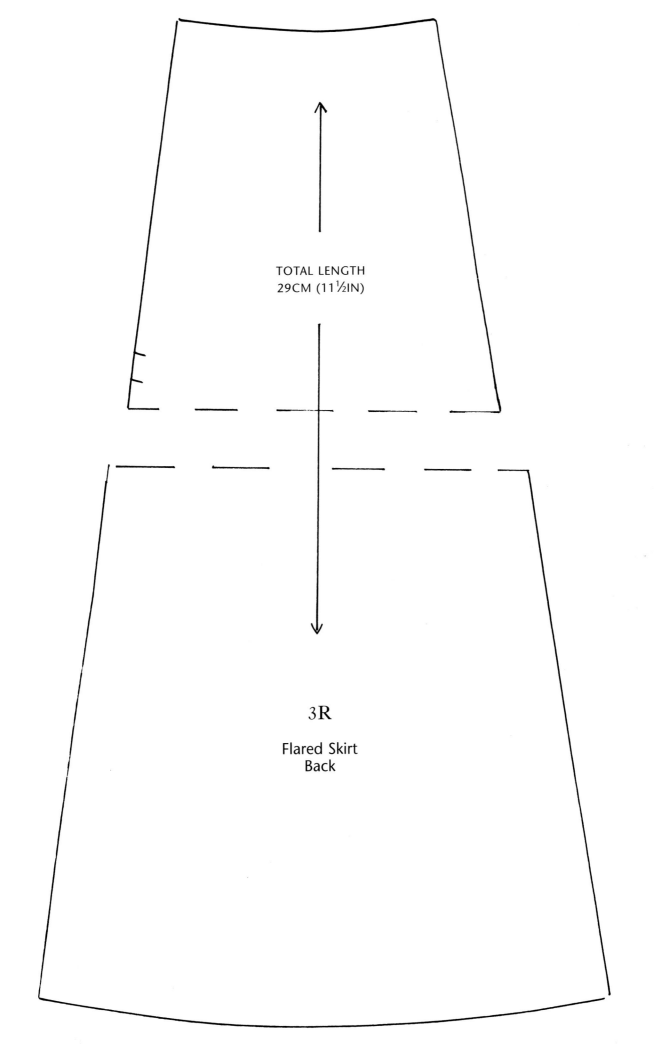

TOTAL LENGTH
29CM (11½IN)

3R

Flared Skirt
Back

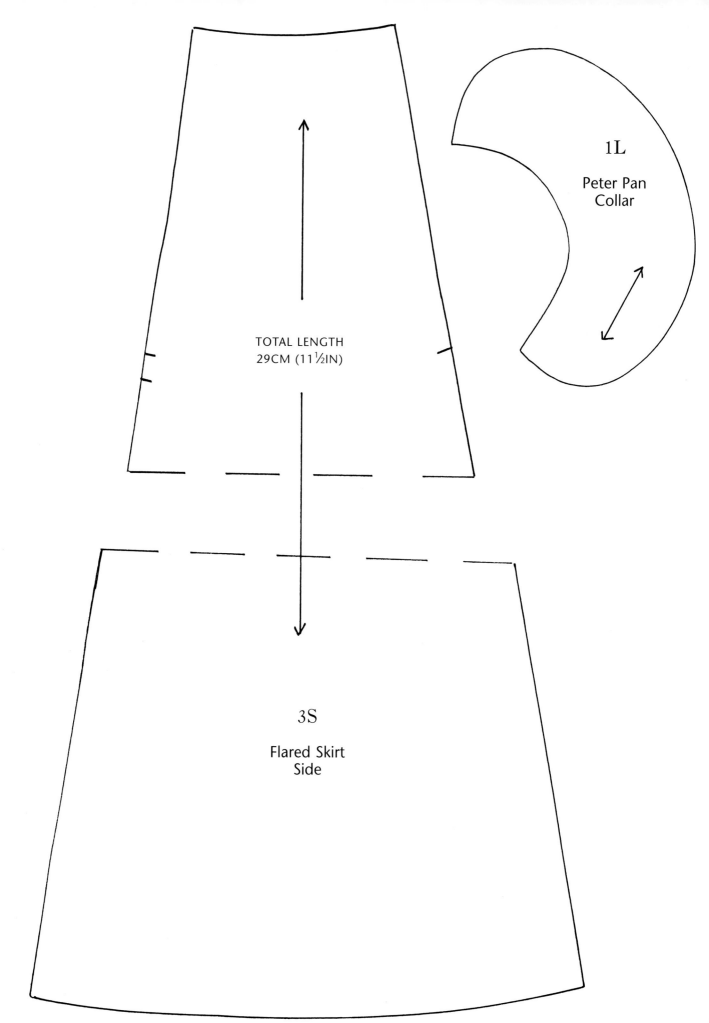

1L

Peter Pan
Collar

TOTAL LENGTH
29CM (11½IN)

3S

Flared Skirt
Side

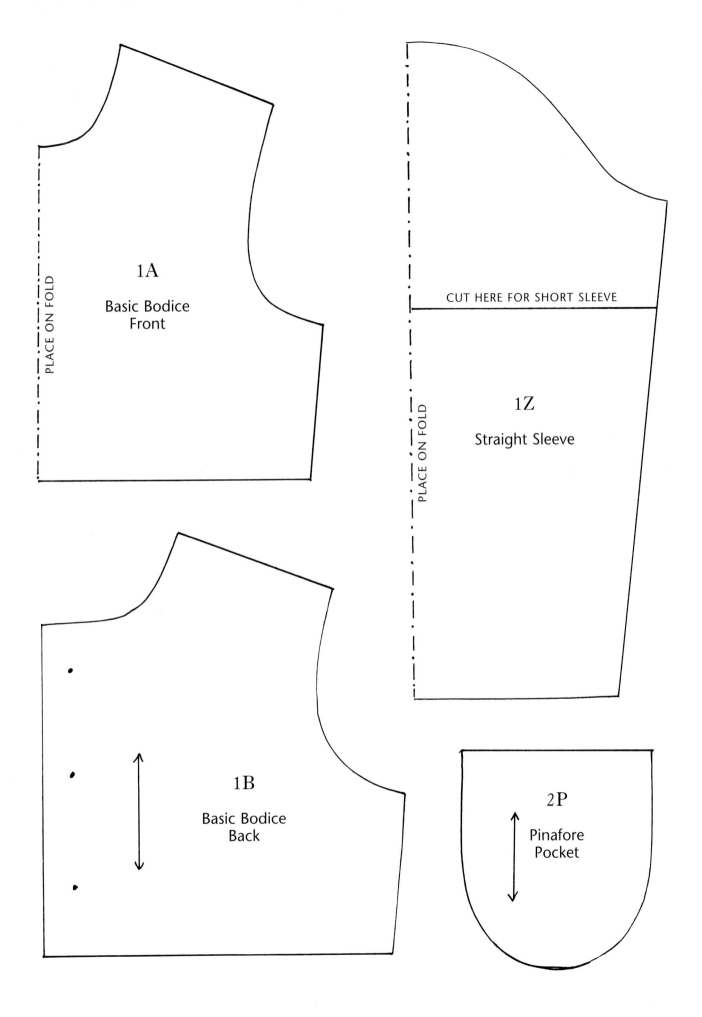

1A

Basic Bodice
Front

PLACE ON FOLD

CUT HERE FOR SHORT SLEEVE

1Z

Straight Sleeve

PLACE ON FOLD

1B

Basic Bodice
Back

2P

Pinafore
Pocket

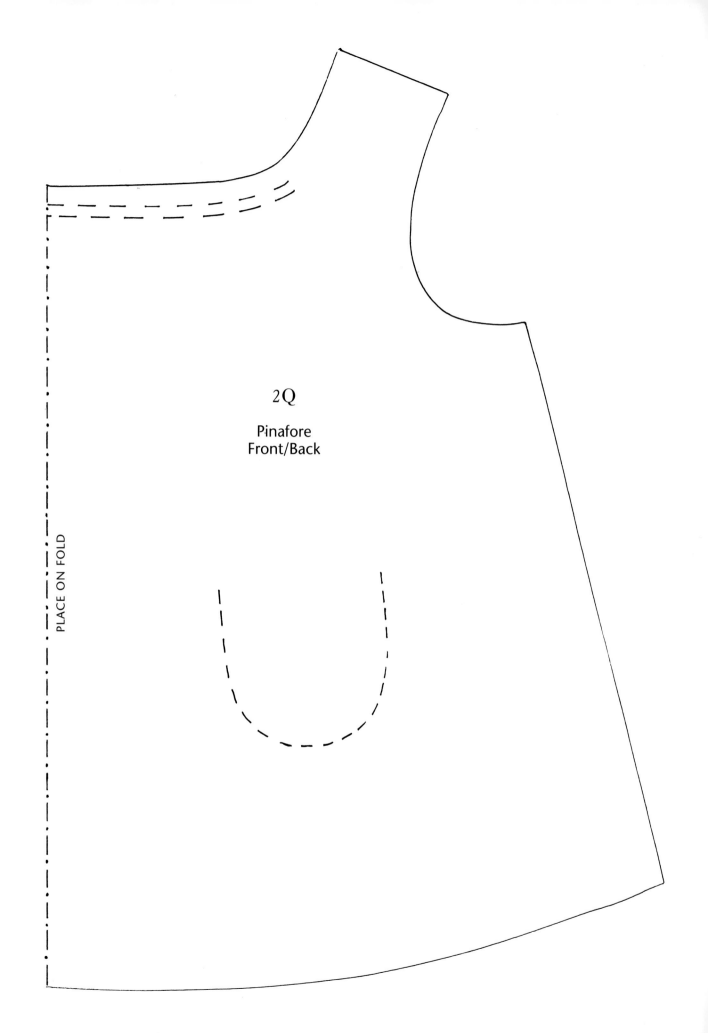

2Q

Pinafore
Front/Back

PLACE ON FOLD

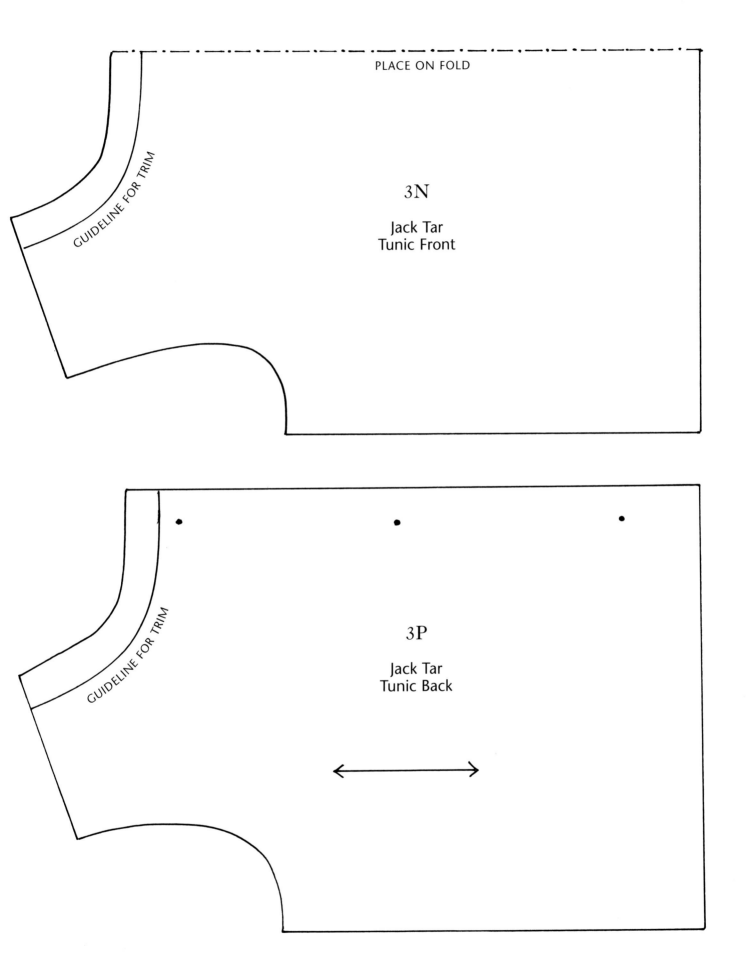

PLACE ON FOLD

GUIDELINE FOR TRIM

3N

Jack Tar
Tunic Front

GUIDELINE FOR TRIM

3P

Jack Tar
Tunic Back

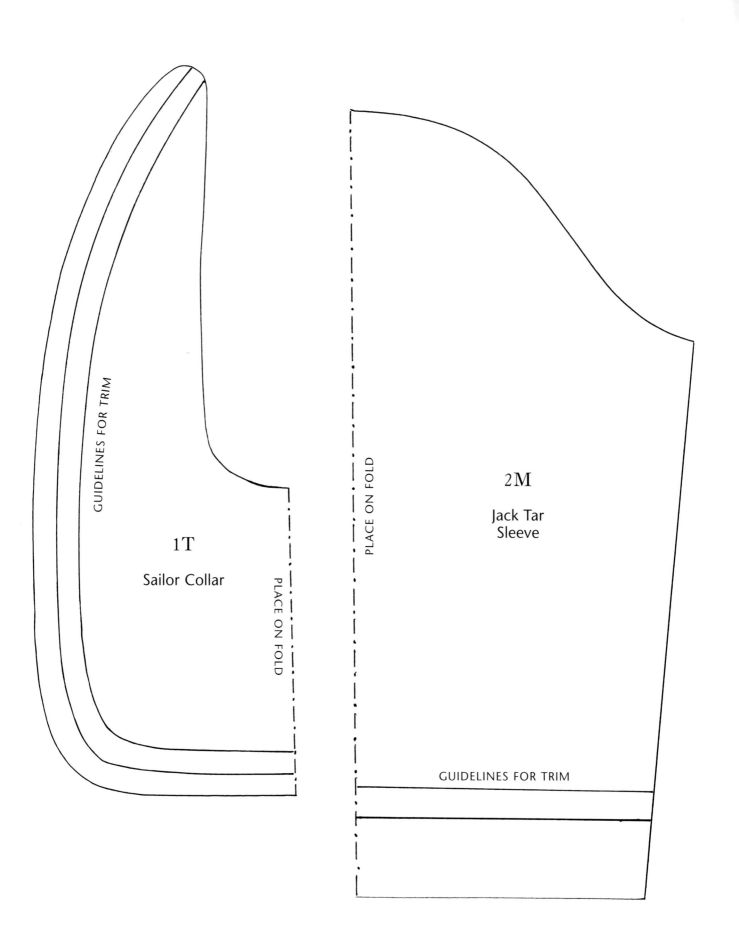

GUIDELINES FOR TRIM

1T

Sailor Collar

PLACE ON FOLD

PLACE ON FOLD

2M

Jack Tar
Sleeve

GUIDELINES FOR TRIM

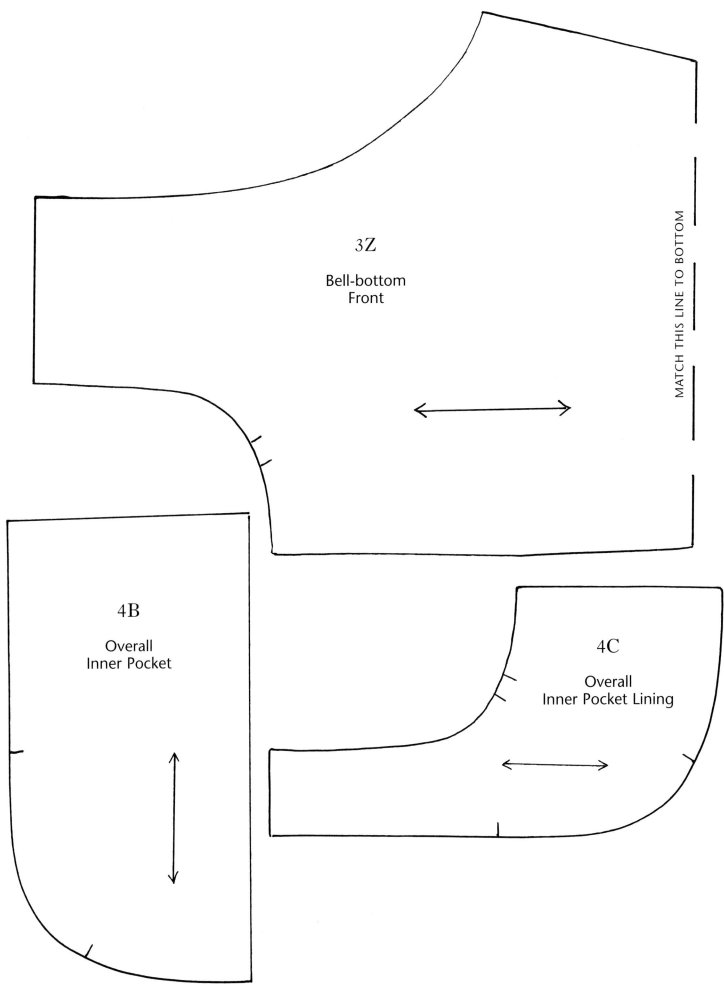

3Z

Bell-bottom
Front

MATCH THIS LINE TO BOTTOM

4B

Overall
Inner Pocket

4C

Overall
Inner Pocket Lining

93

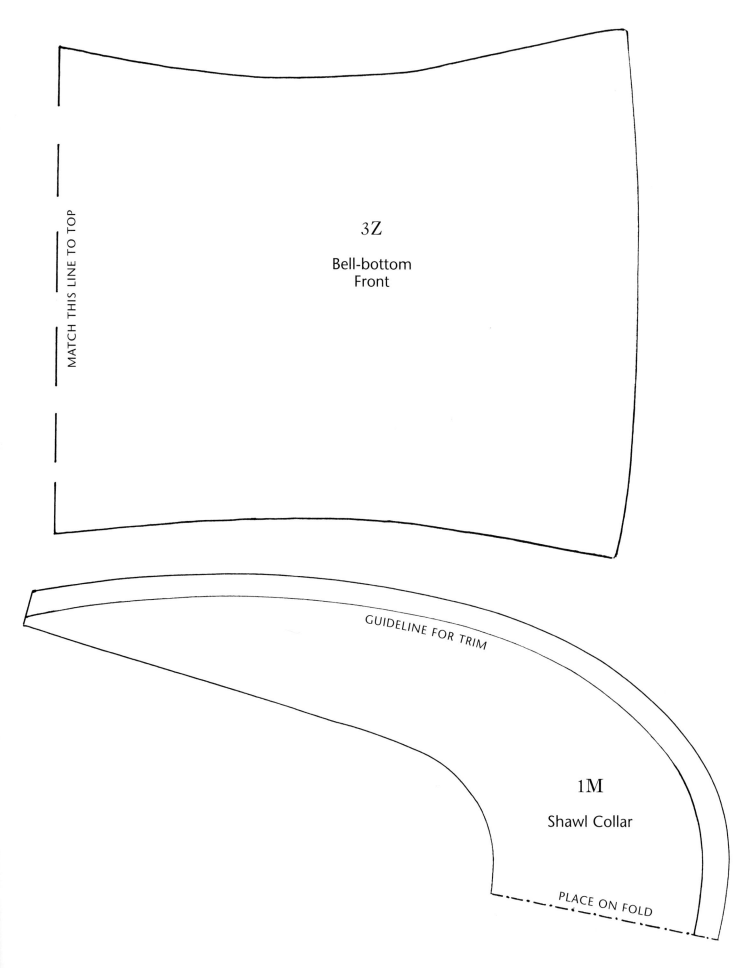

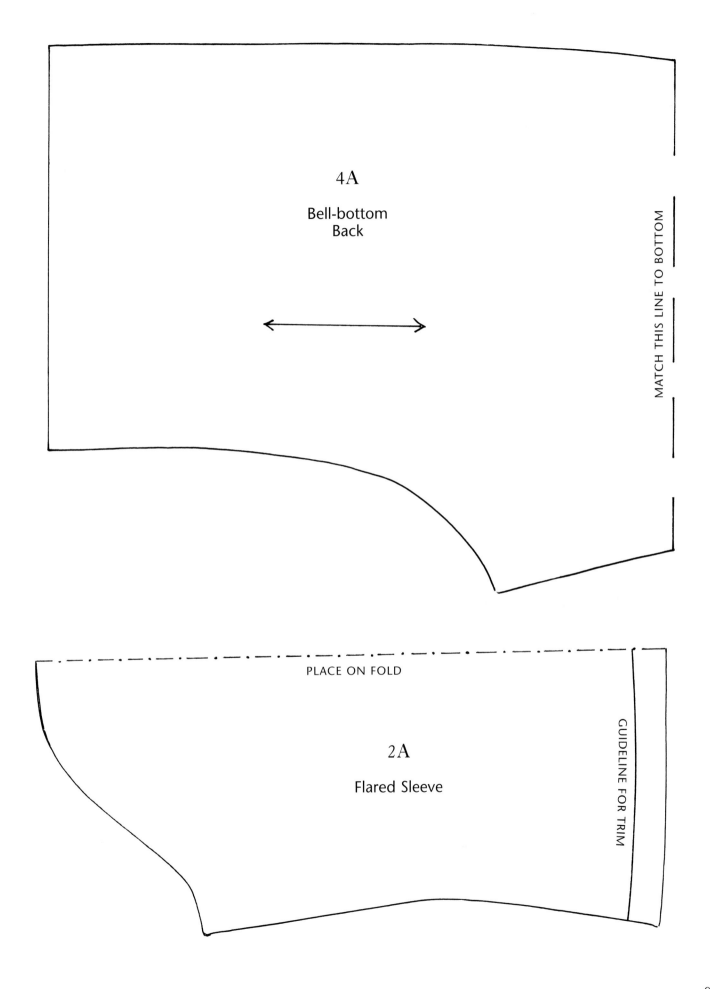

4A

Bell-bottom
Back

MATCH THIS LINE TO BOTTOM

PLACE ON FOLD

2A

Flared Sleeve

GUIDELINE FOR TRIM

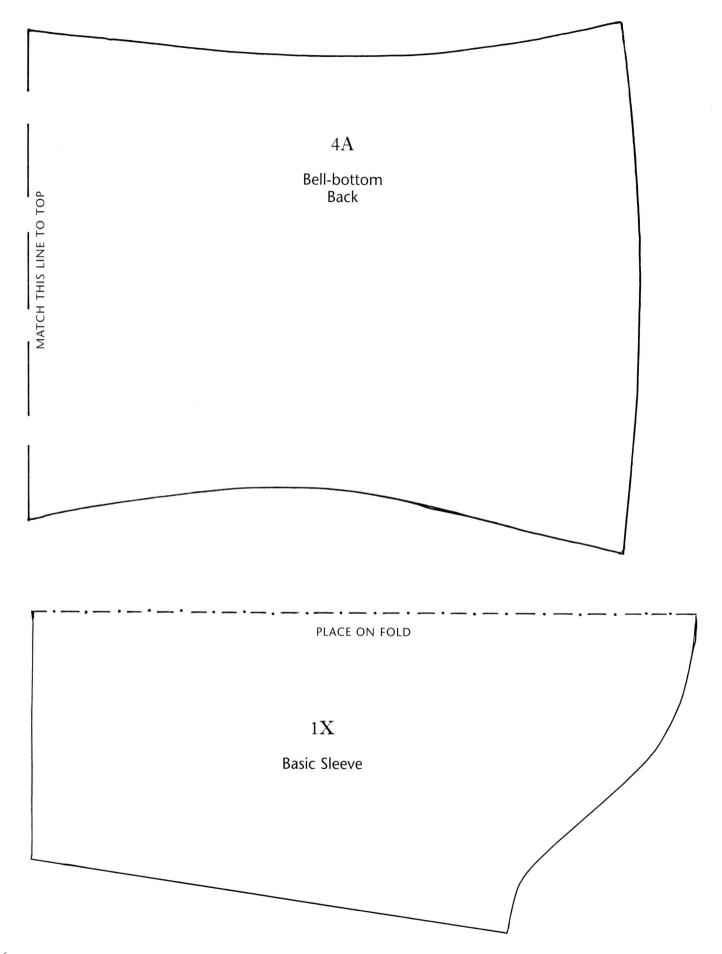

4A

Bell-bottom
Back

MATCH THIS LINE TO TOP

PLACE ON FOLD

1X

Basic Sleeve

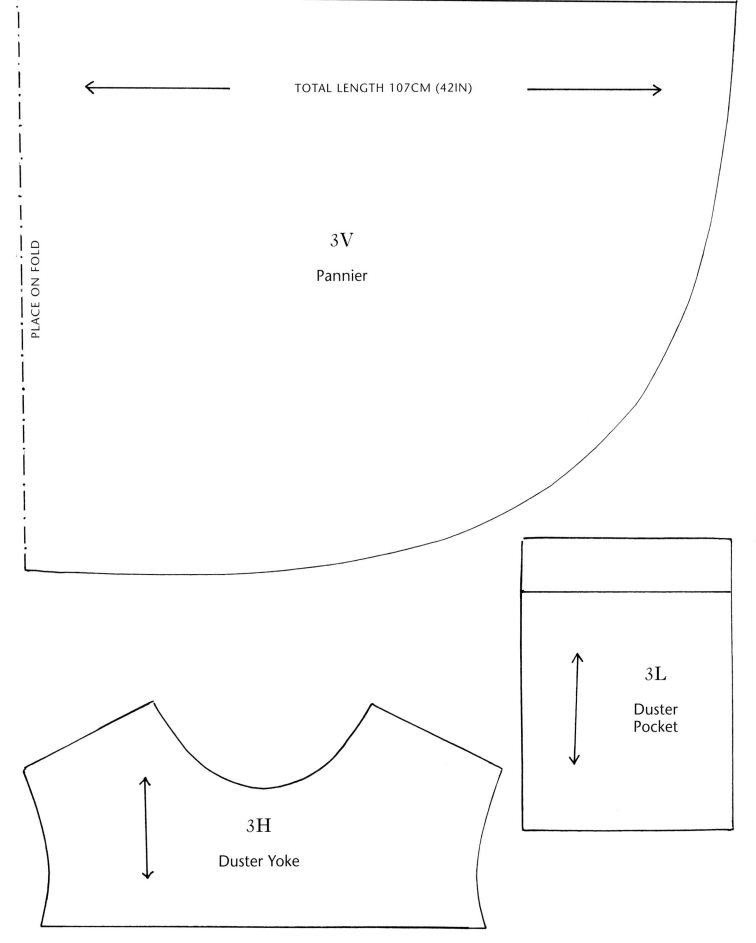

PLACE ON FOLD

TOTAL LENGTH 107CM (42IN)

3V

Pannier

3L

Duster
Pocket

3H

Duster Yoke

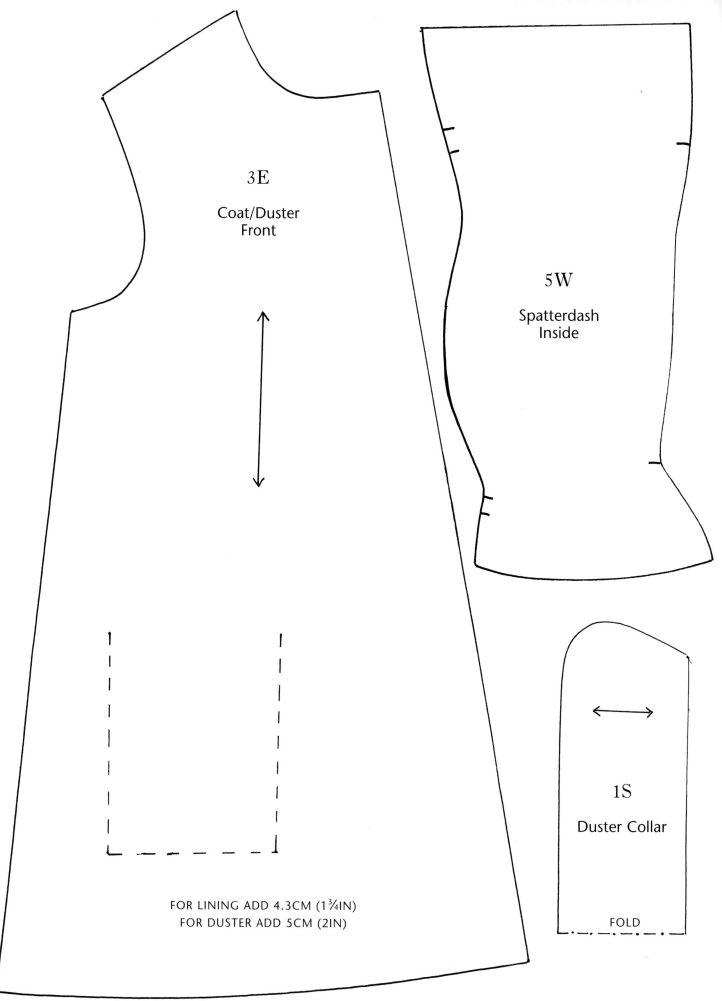

3E

Coat/Duster
Front

5W

Spatterdash
Inside

1S

Duster Collar

FOLD

FOR LINING ADD 4.3CM (1¾IN)
FOR DUSTER ADD 5CM (2IN)

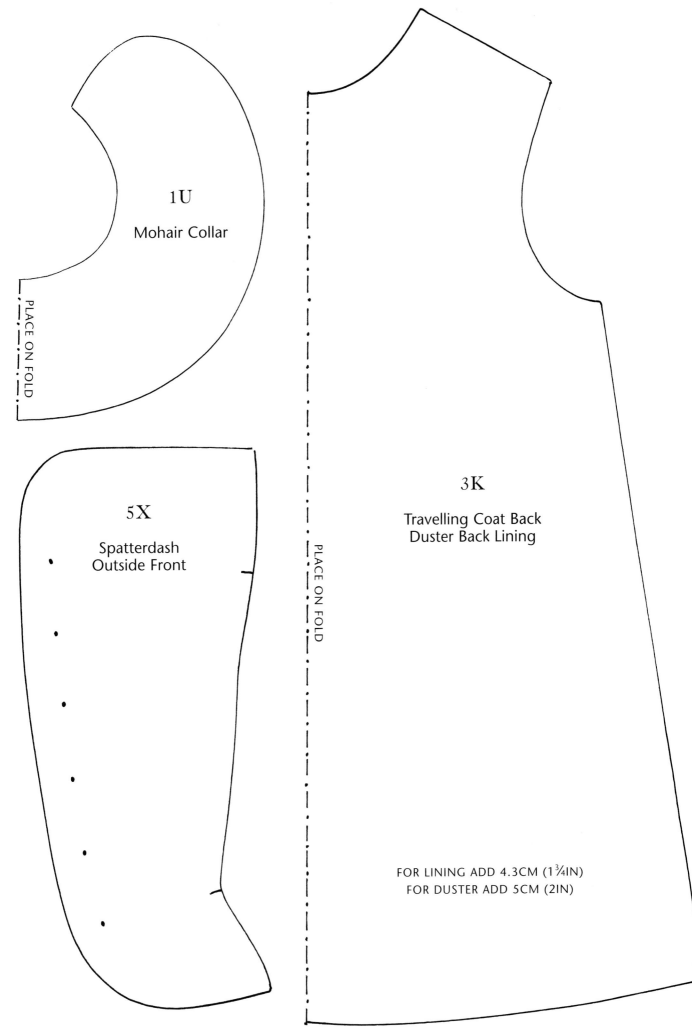

1U

Mohair Collar

PLACE ON FOLD

5X

Spatterdash
Outside Front

PLACE ON FOLD

3K

Travelling Coat Back
Duster Back Lining

FOR LINING ADD 4.3CM (1¾IN)
FOR DUSTER ADD 5CM (2IN)

99

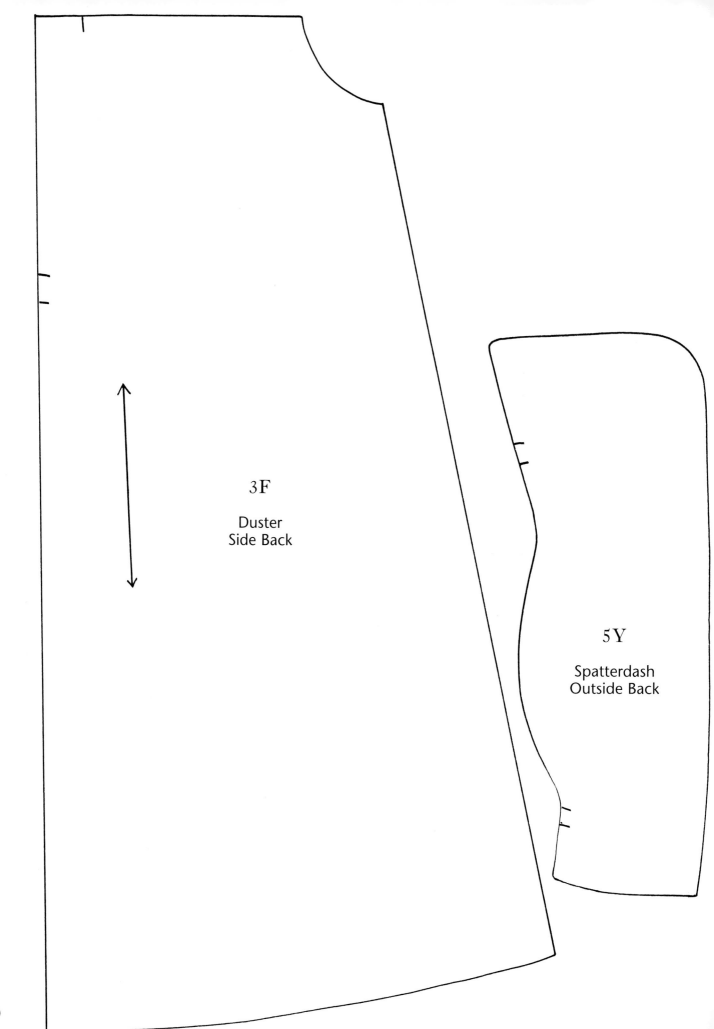

3F

Duster
Side Back

5Y

Spatterdash
Outside Back

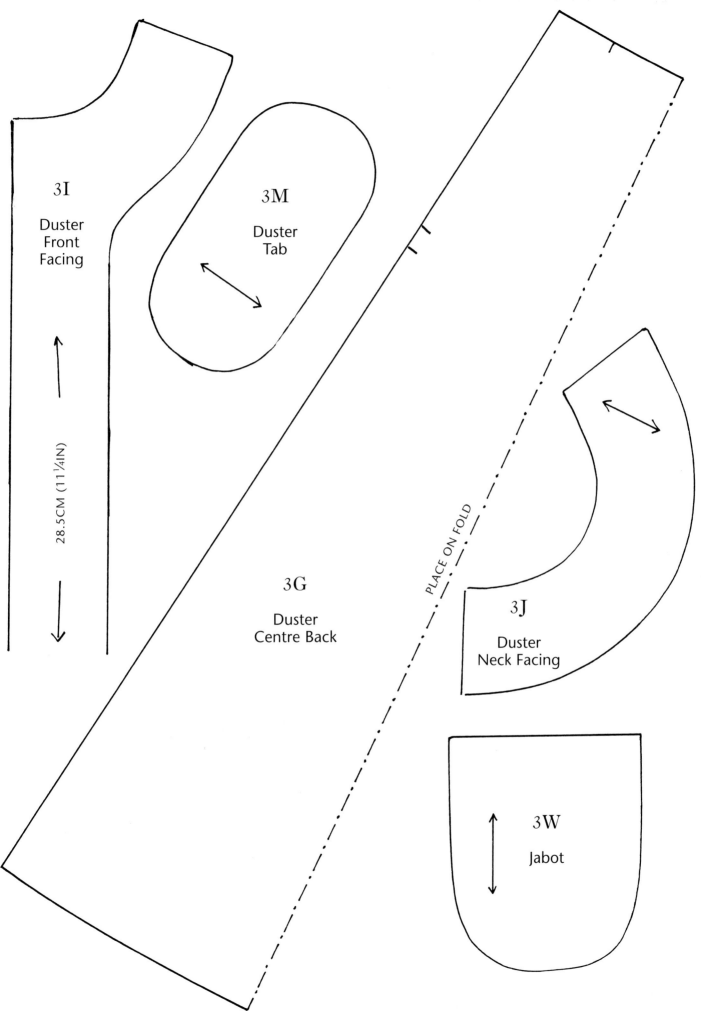

3I

Duster
Front
Facing

28.5CM (11¼IN)

3M

Duster
Tab

3G

Duster
Centre Back

PLACE ON FOLD

3J

Duster
Neck Facing

3W

Jabot

101

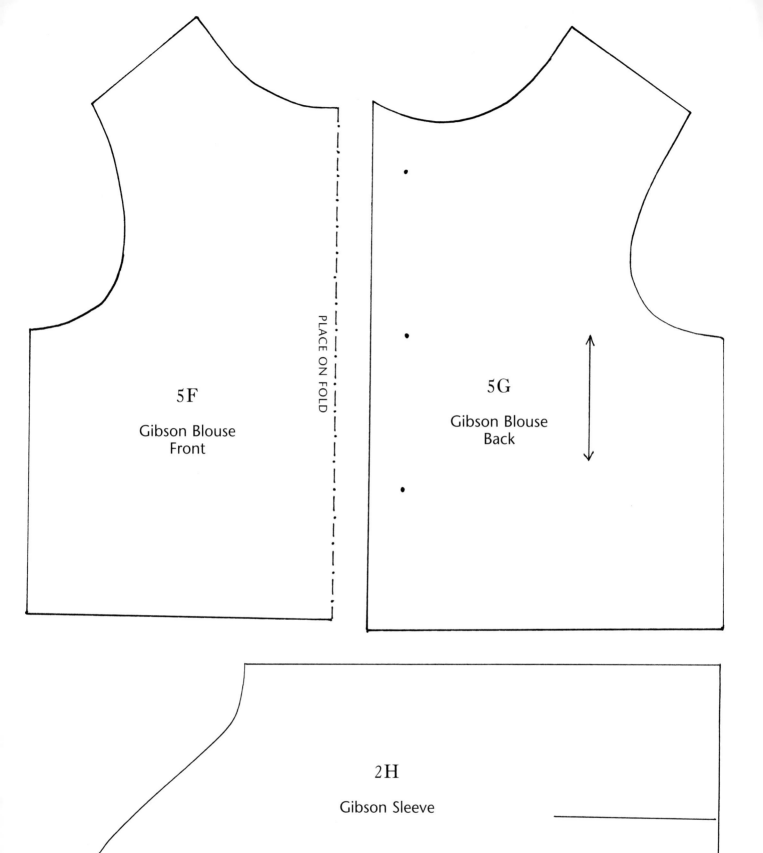

5F

Gibson Blouse
Front

PLACE ON FOLD

5G

Gibson Blouse
Back

2H

Gibson Sleeve

PLACE ON FOLD

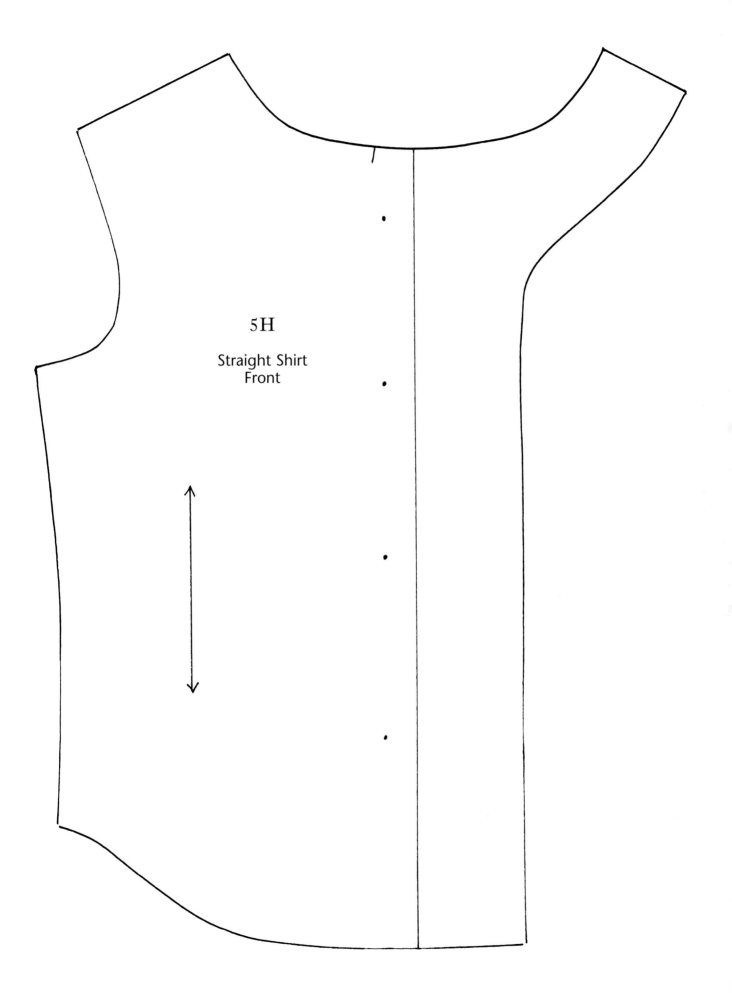

5H

Straight Shirt
Front

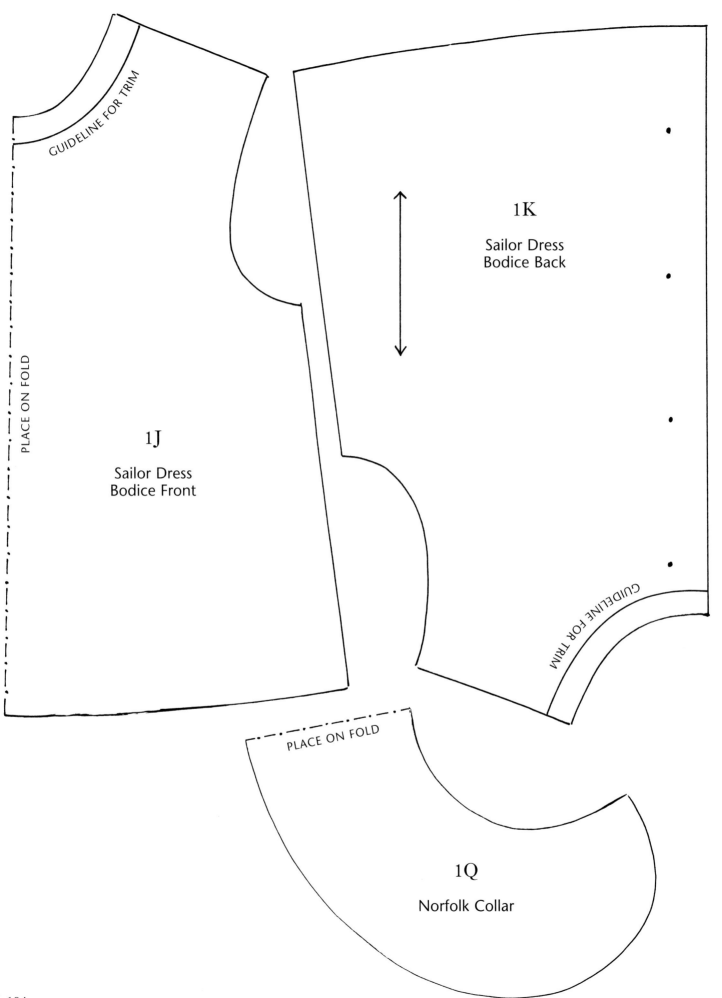

GUIDELINE FOR TRIM

PLACE ON FOLD

1J

Sailor Dress
Bodice Front

1K

Sailor Dress
Bodice Back

GUIDELINE FOR TRIM

PLACE ON FOLD

1Q

Norfolk Collar

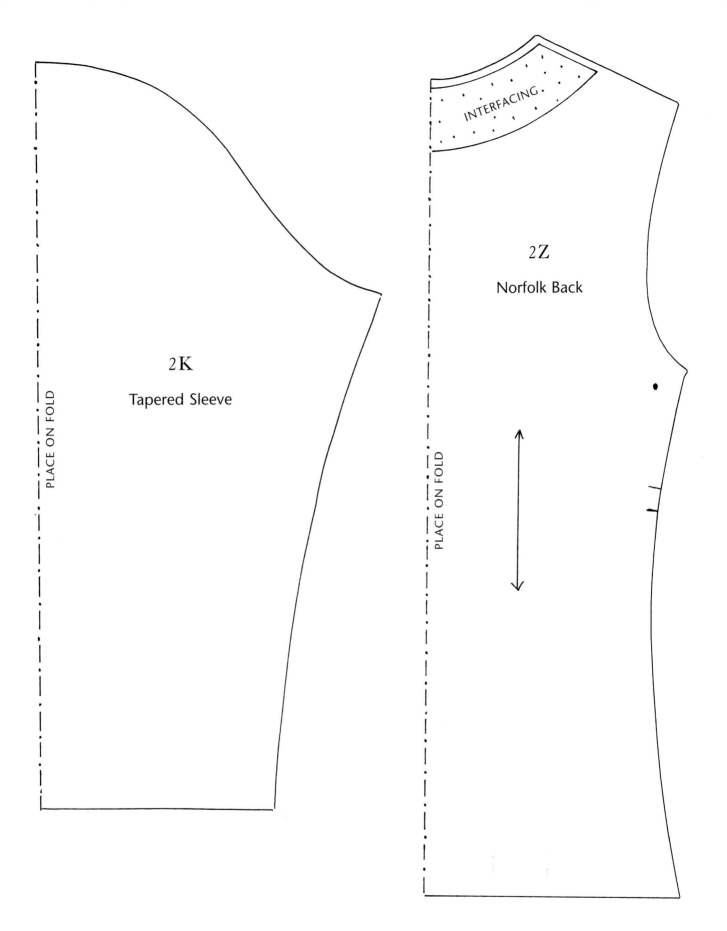

2K

Tapered Sleeve

PLACE ON FOLD

INTERFACING

2Z

Norfolk Back

PLACE ON FOLD

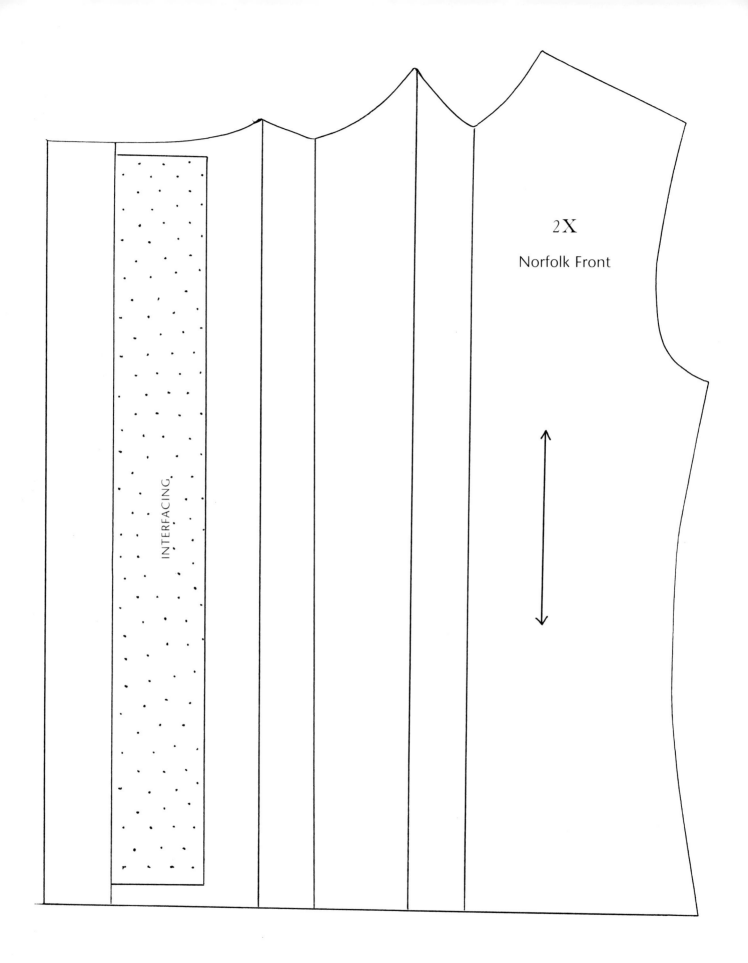

INTERFACING.

2**X**

Norfolk Front

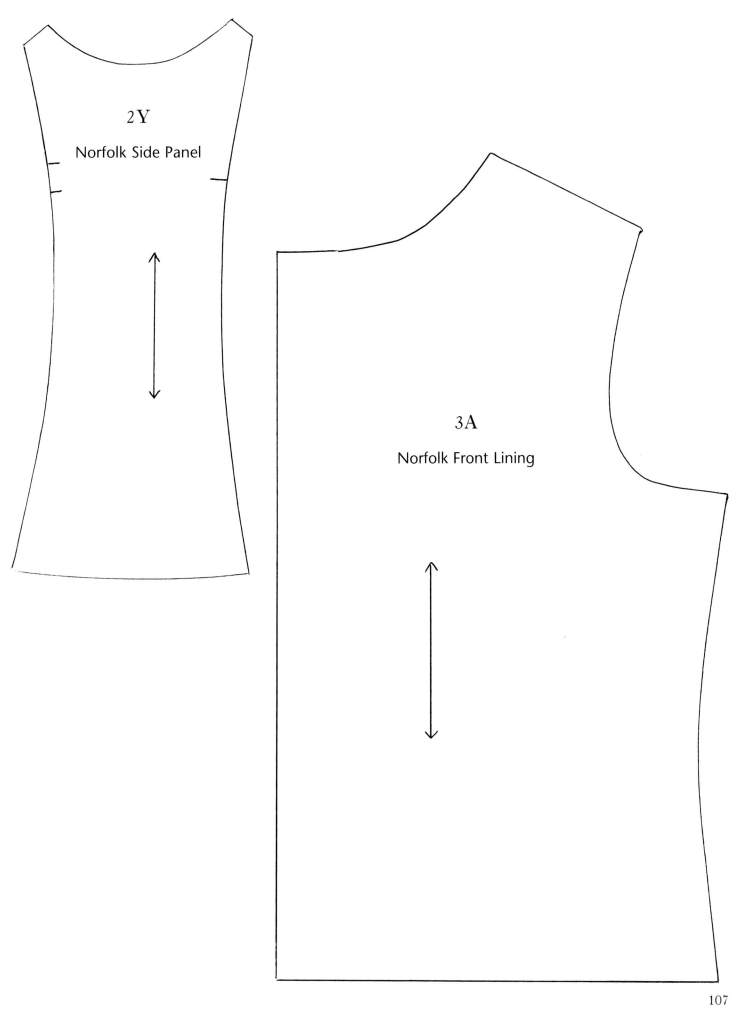

2Y

Norfolk Side Panel

3A

Norfolk Front Lining

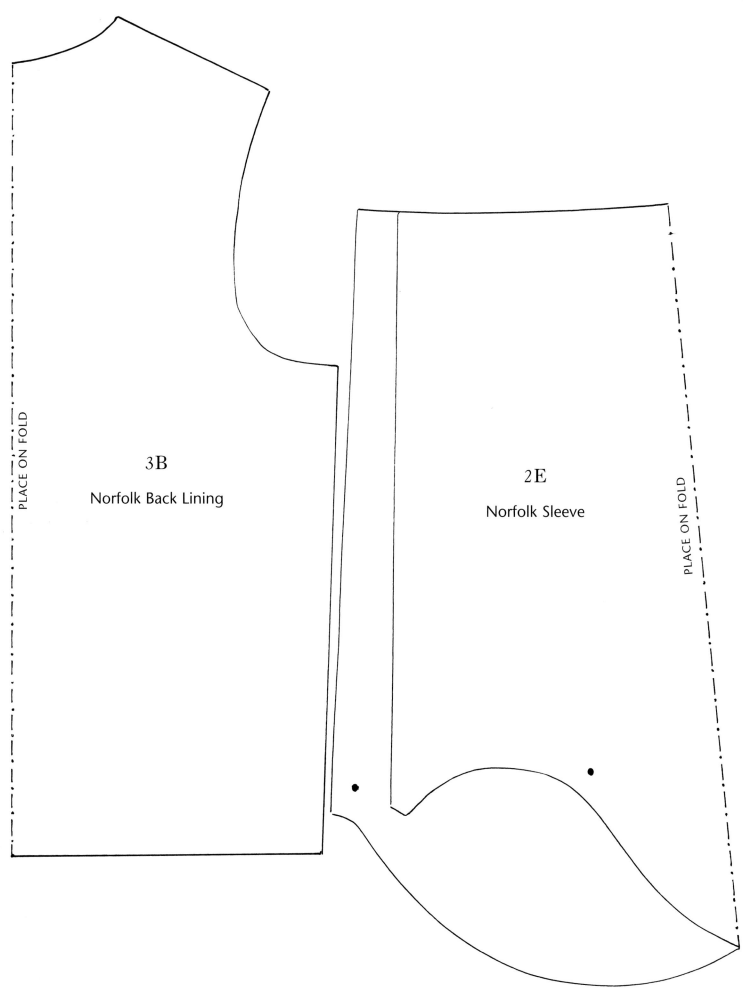

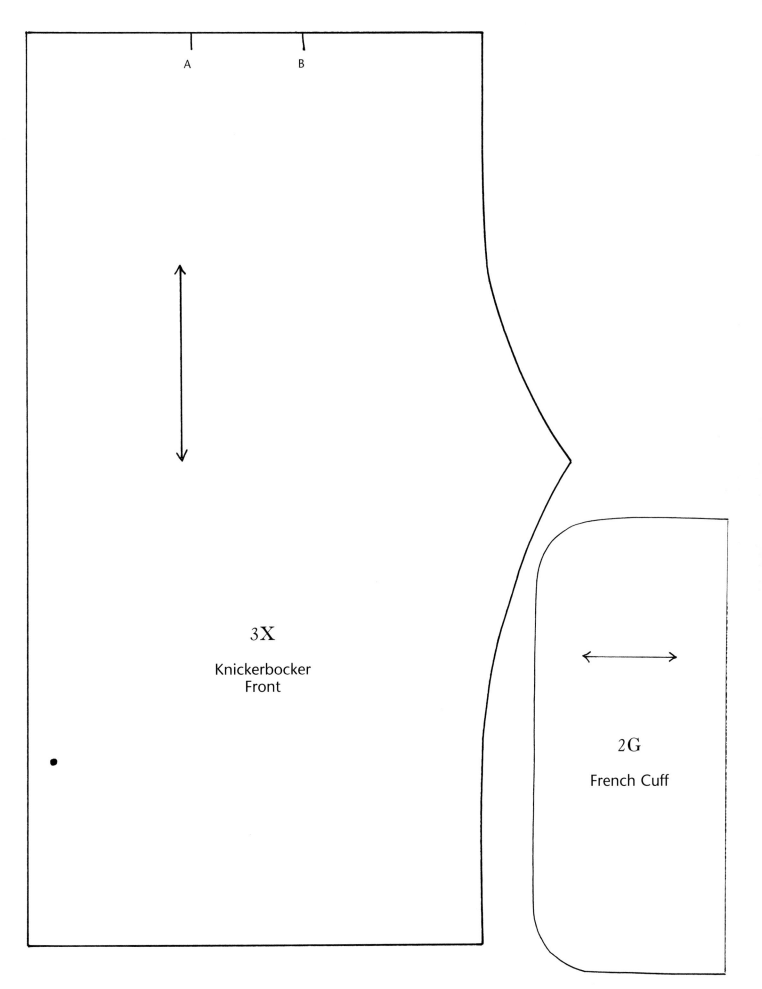

A   B

3X

Knickerbocker
Front

2G

French Cuff

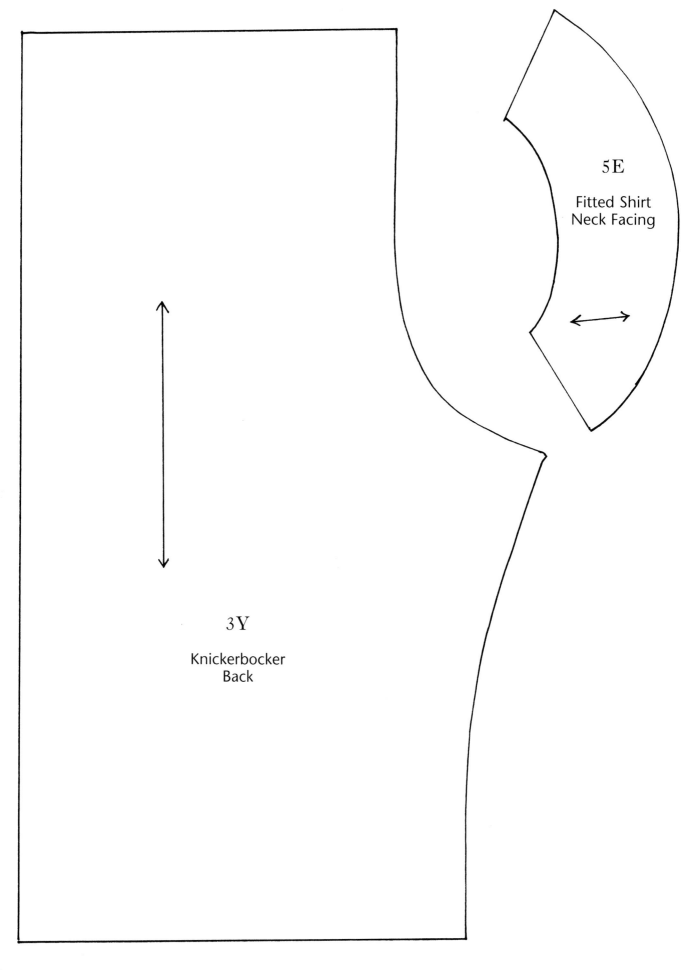

5E

Fitted Shirt
Neck Facing

3Y

Knickerbocker
Back

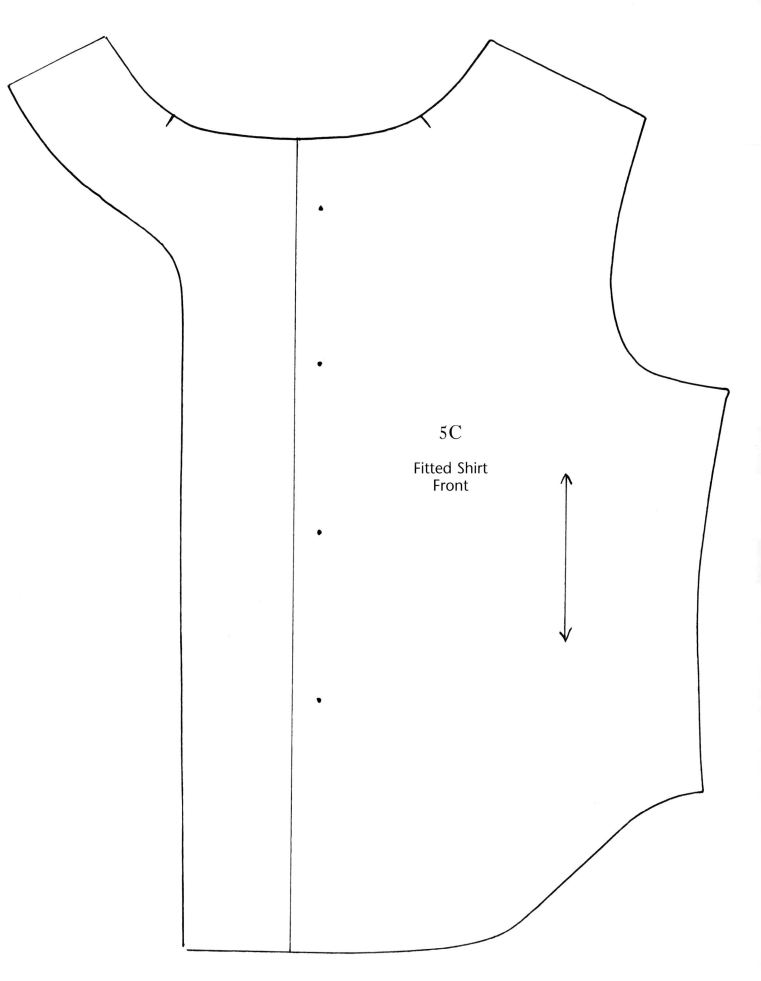

5C

Fitted Shirt
Front

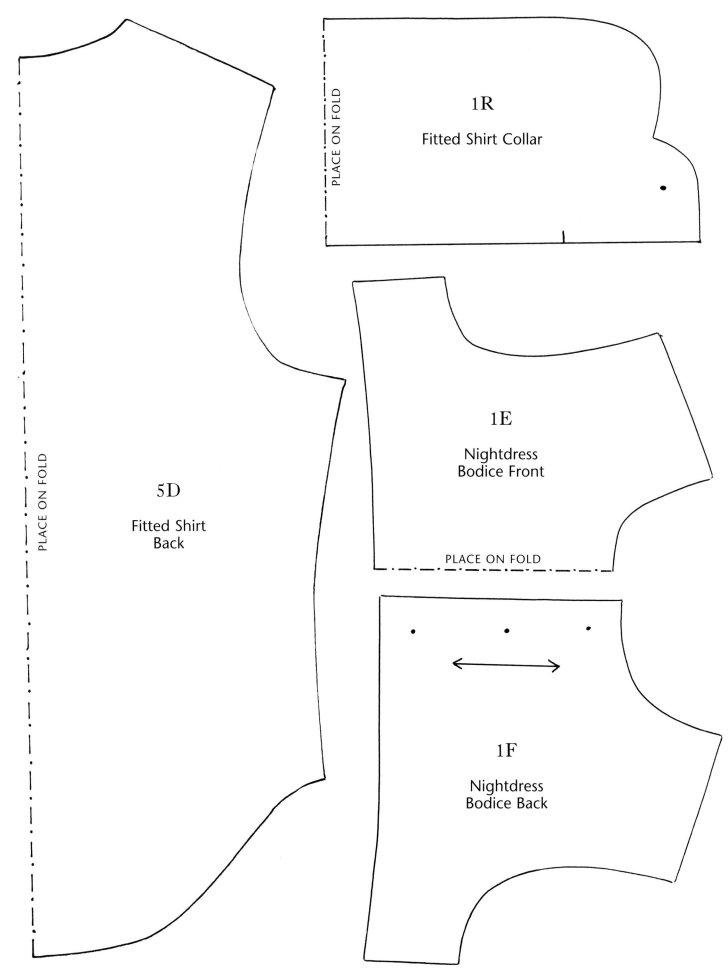

PLACE ON FOLD

1R

Fitted Shirt Collar

PLACE ON FOLD

5D

Fitted Shirt
Back

1E

Nightdress
Bodice Front

PLACE ON FOLD

1F

Nightdress
Bodice Back

112

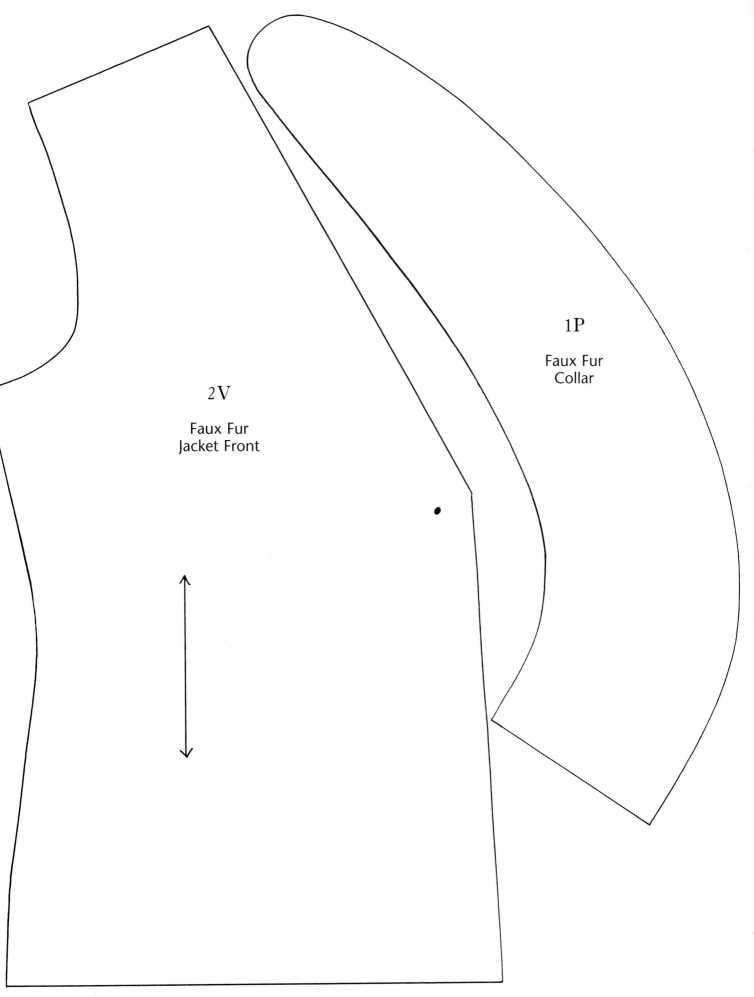

2V

Faux Fur
Jacket Front

1P

Faux Fur
Collar

113

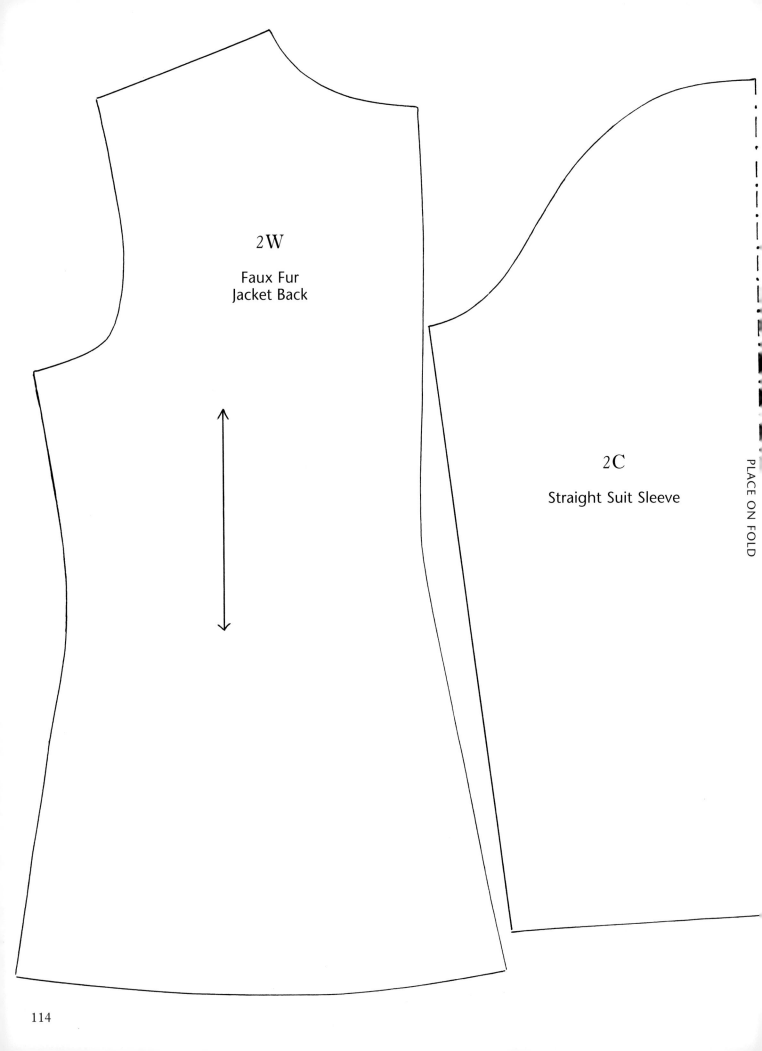

2W

Faux Fur
Jacket Back

2C

Straight Suit Sleeve

PLACE ON FOLD

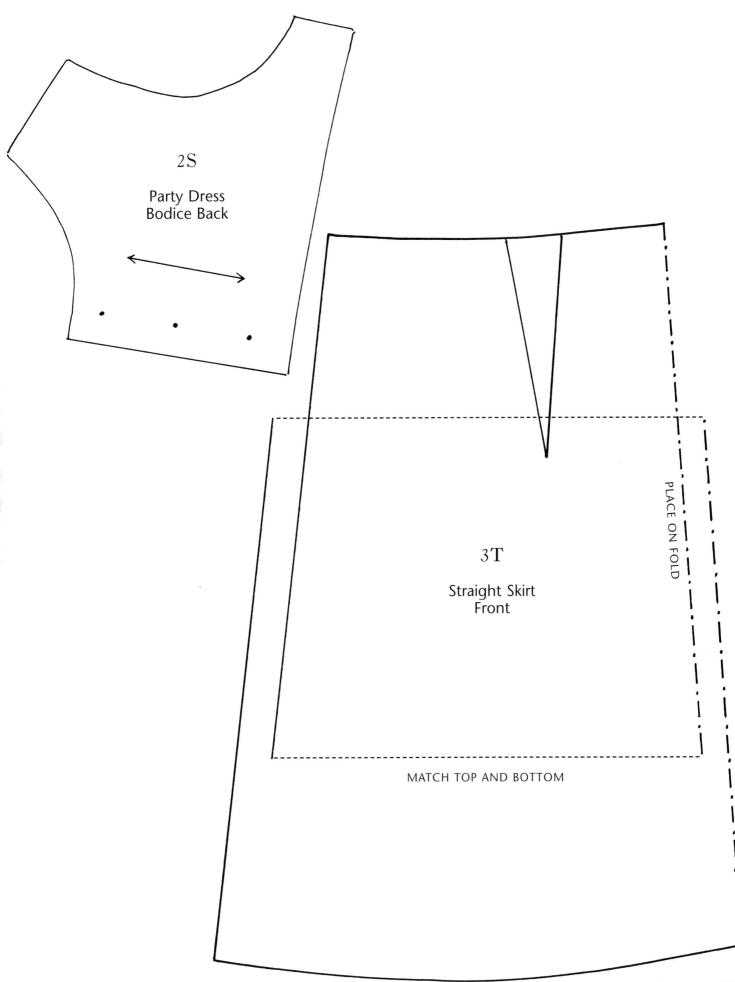

2S

Party Dress
Bodice Back

3T

Straight Skirt
Front

PLACE ON FOLD

MATCH TOP AND BOTTOM

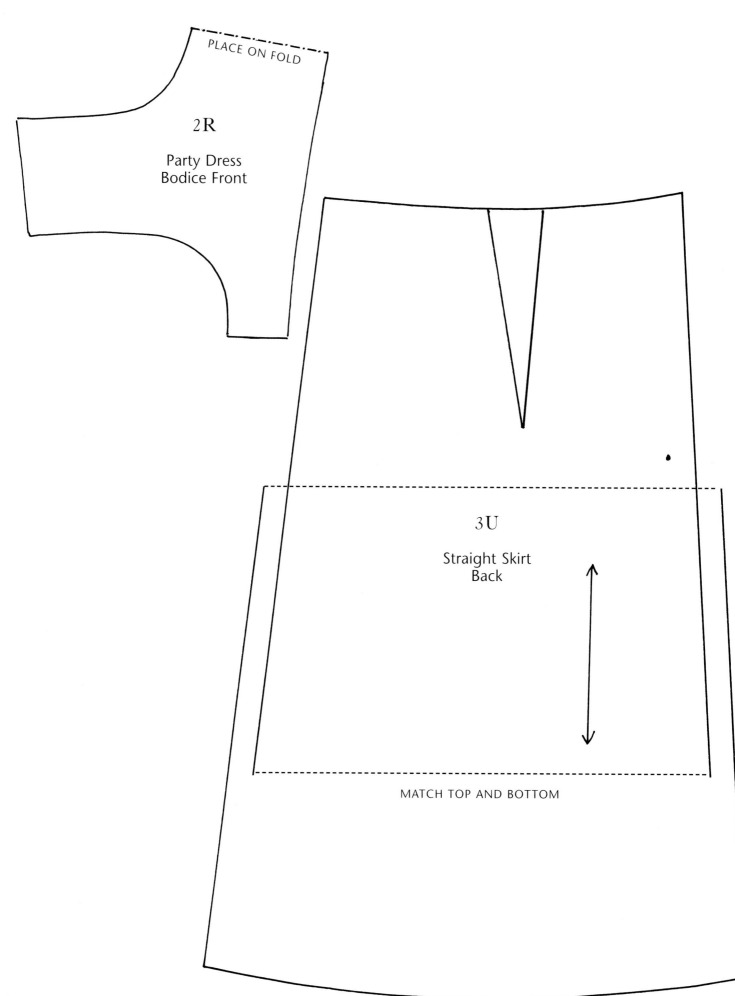

PLACE ON FOLD

2R

Party Dress
Bodice Front

3U

Straight Skirt
Back

MATCH TOP AND BOTTOM

PLACE ON FOLD

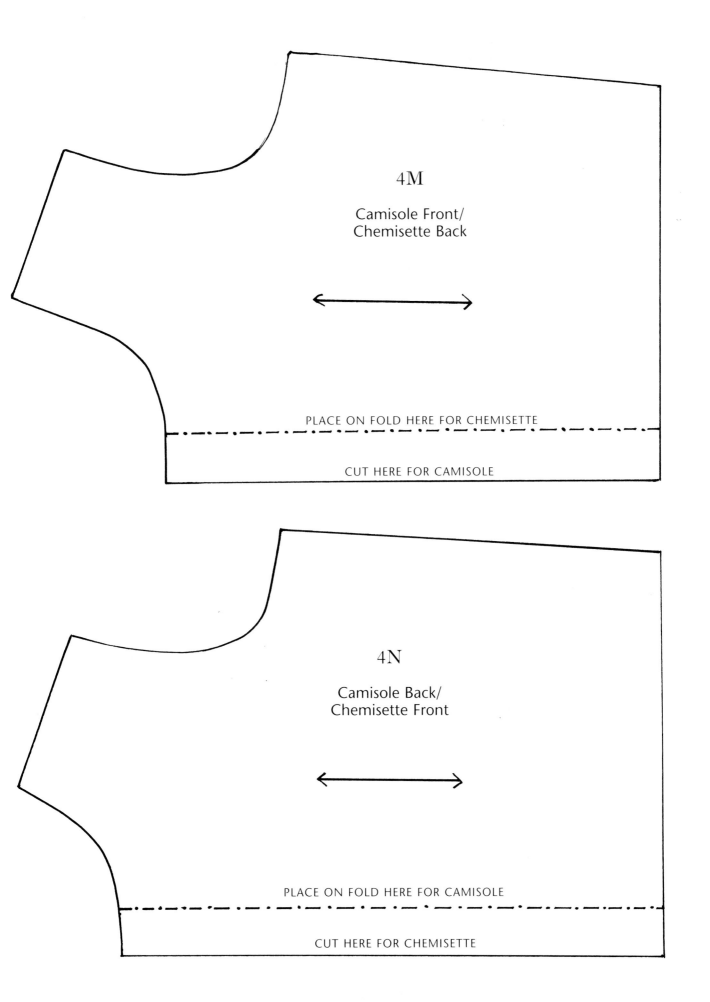

4M

Camisole Front/
Chemisette Back

PLACE ON FOLD HERE FOR CHEMISETTE

CUT HERE FOR CAMISOLE

4N

Camisole Back/
Chemisette Front

PLACE ON FOLD HERE FOR CAMISOLE

CUT HERE FOR CHEMISETTE

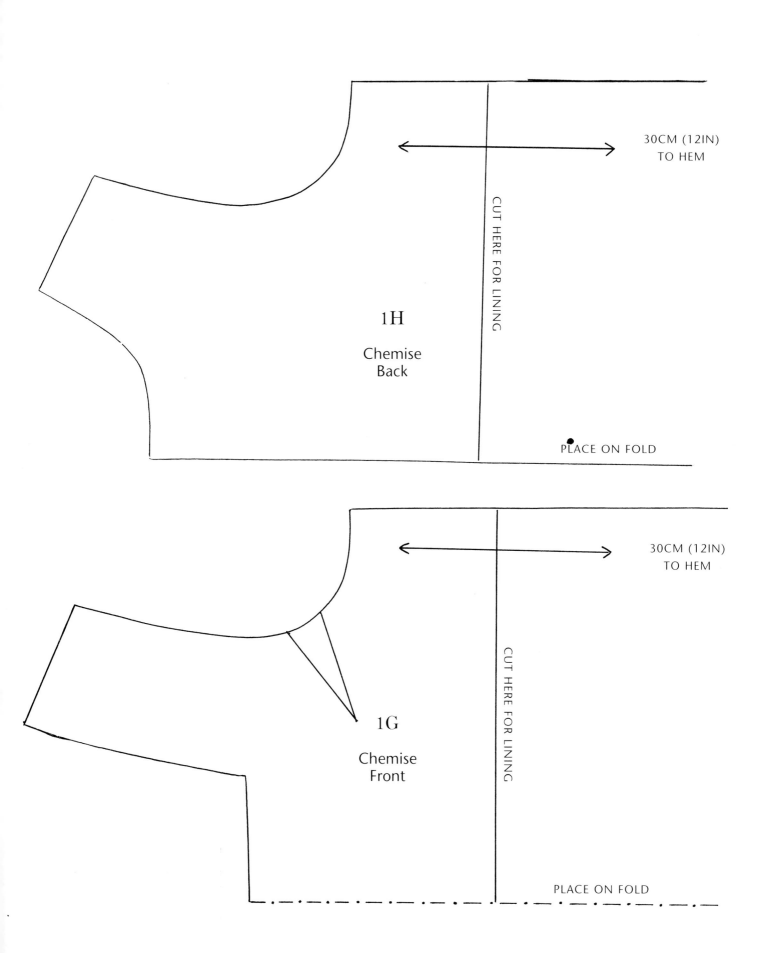

30CM (12IN)
TO HEM

CUT HERE FOR LINING

1H

Chemise
Back

PLACE ON FOLD

30CM (12IN)
TO HEM

CUT HERE FOR LINING

1G

Chemise
Front

PLACE ON FOLD

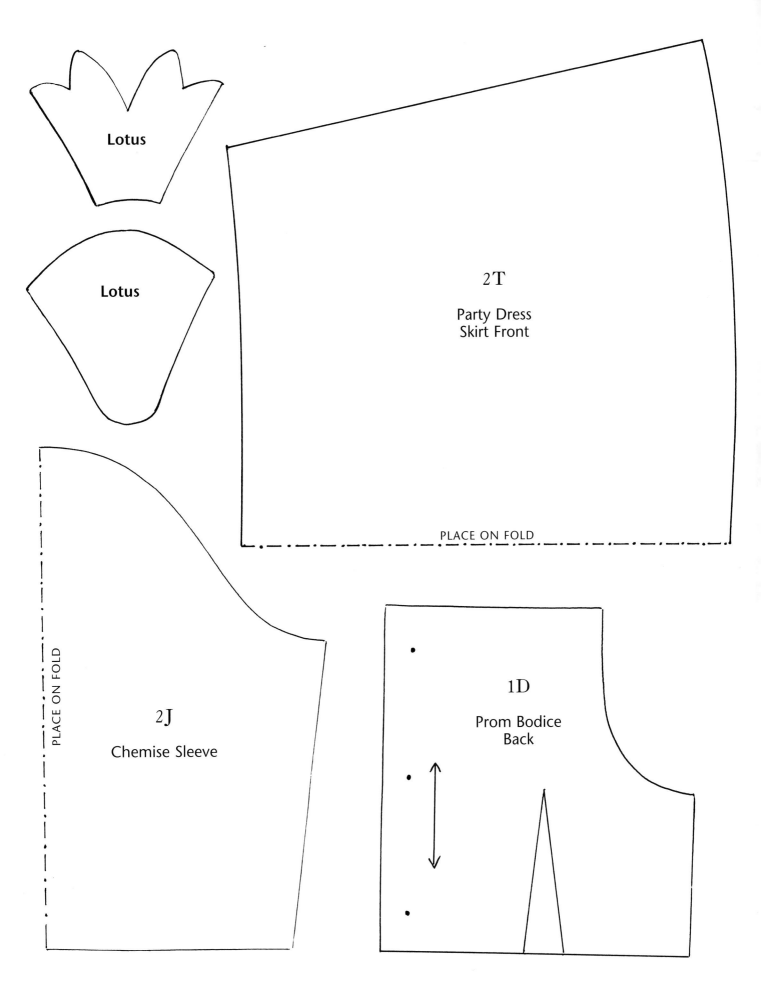

Lotus

Lotus

2T

Party Dress
Skirt Front

PLACE ON FOLD

PLACE ON FOLD

2J

Chemise Sleeve

1D

Prom Bodice
Back

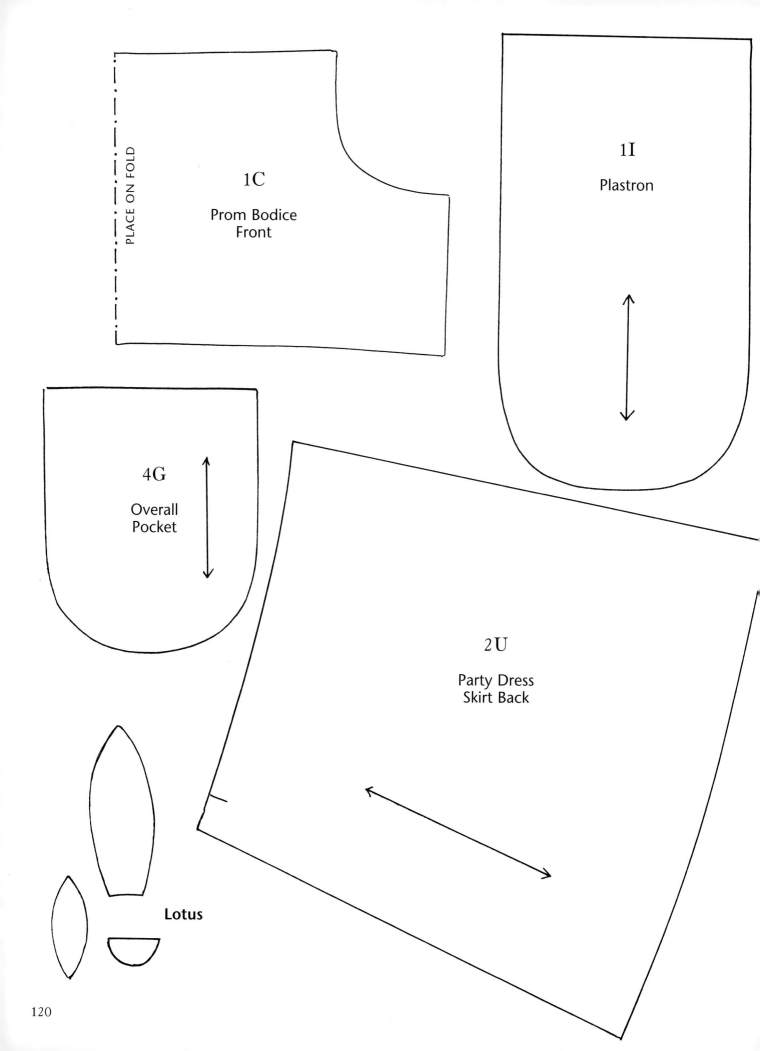

PLACE ON FOLD

1C

Prom Bodice
Front

1I

Plastron

4G

Overall
Pocket

2U

Party Dress
Skirt Back

Lotus

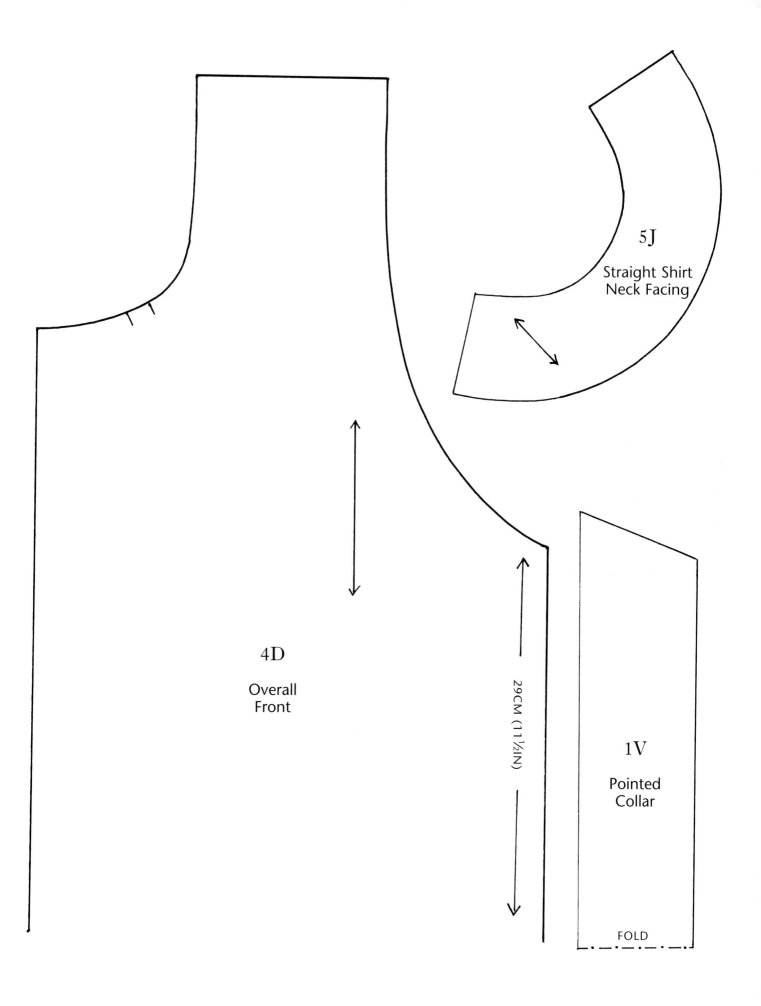

5J

Straight Shirt
Neck Facing

4D

Overall
Front

29CM (11½IN)

1V

Pointed
Collar

FOLD

121

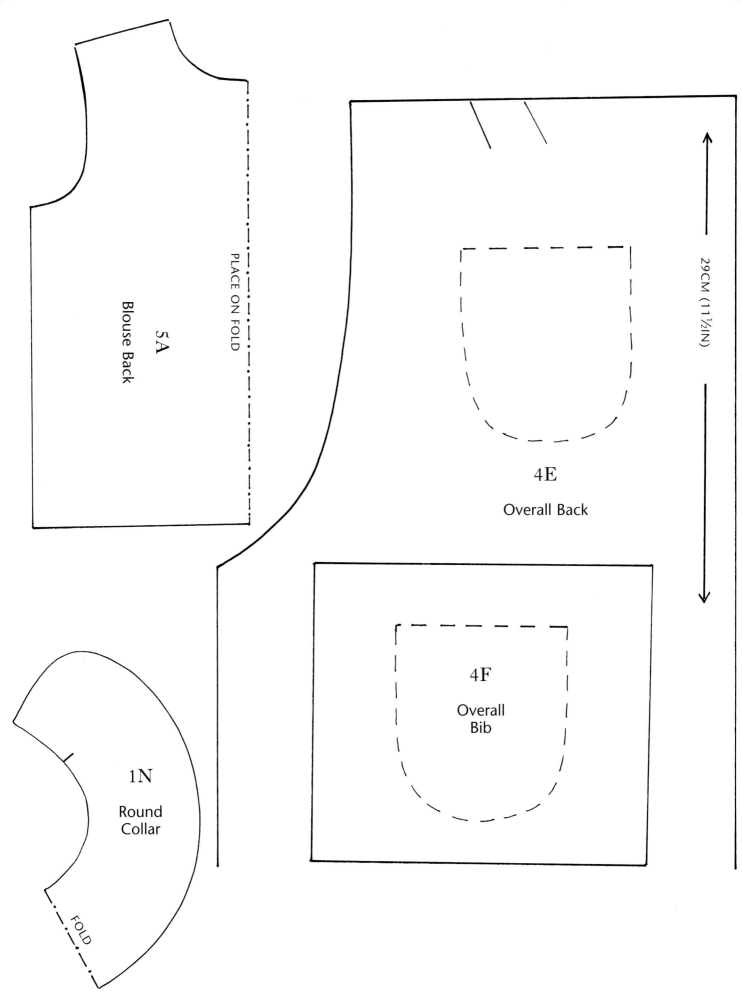

PLACE ON FOLD

5A

Blouse Back

29CM (11½IN)

4E

Overall Back

4F

Overall
Bib

1N

Round
Collar

FOLD

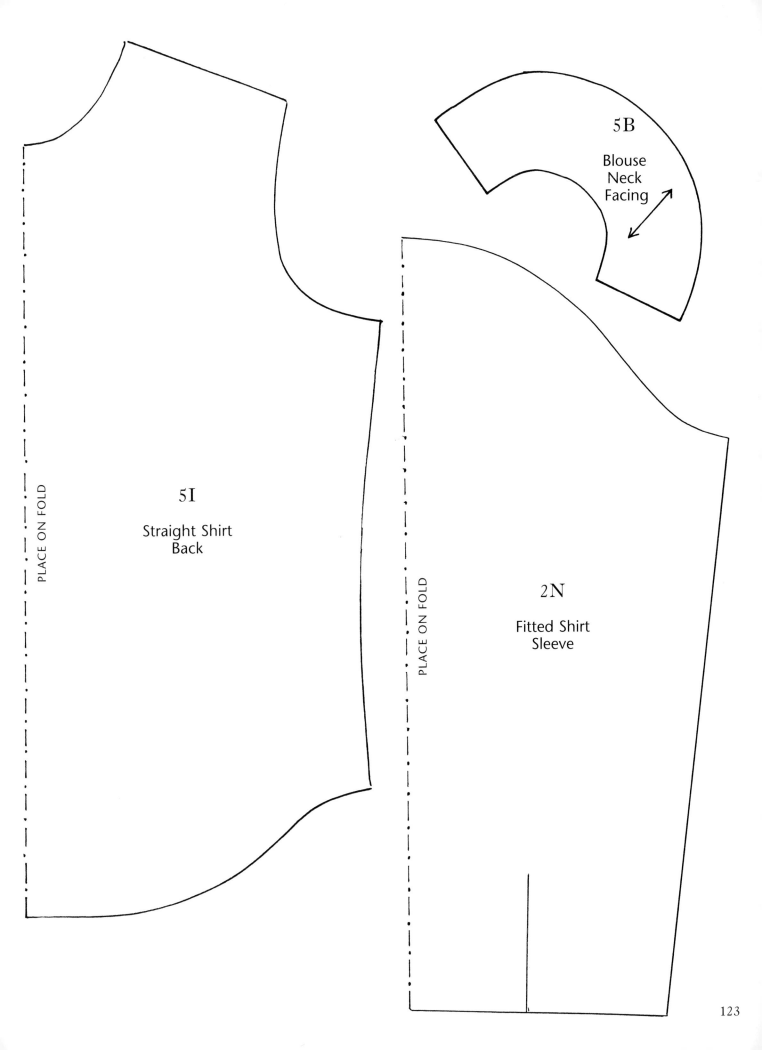

PLACE ON FOLD

5I

Straight Shirt
Back

5B

Blouse
Neck
Facing

PLACE ON FOLD

2N

Fitted Shirt
Sleeve

123

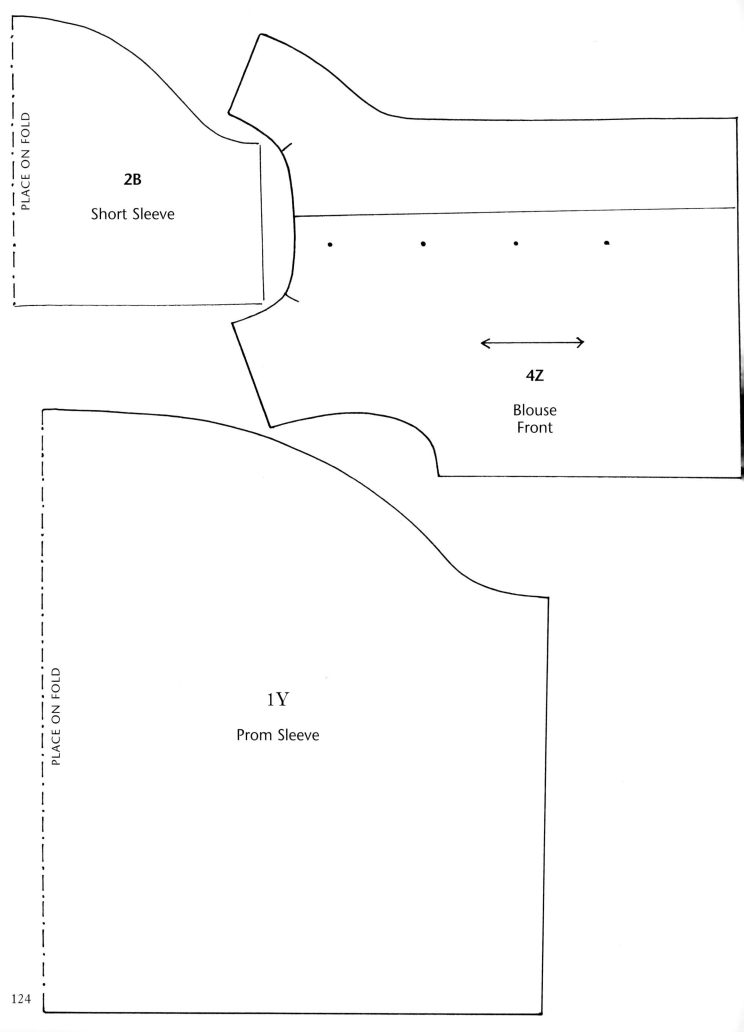

2B

Short Sleeve

4Z

Blouse
Front

1Y

Prom Sleeve

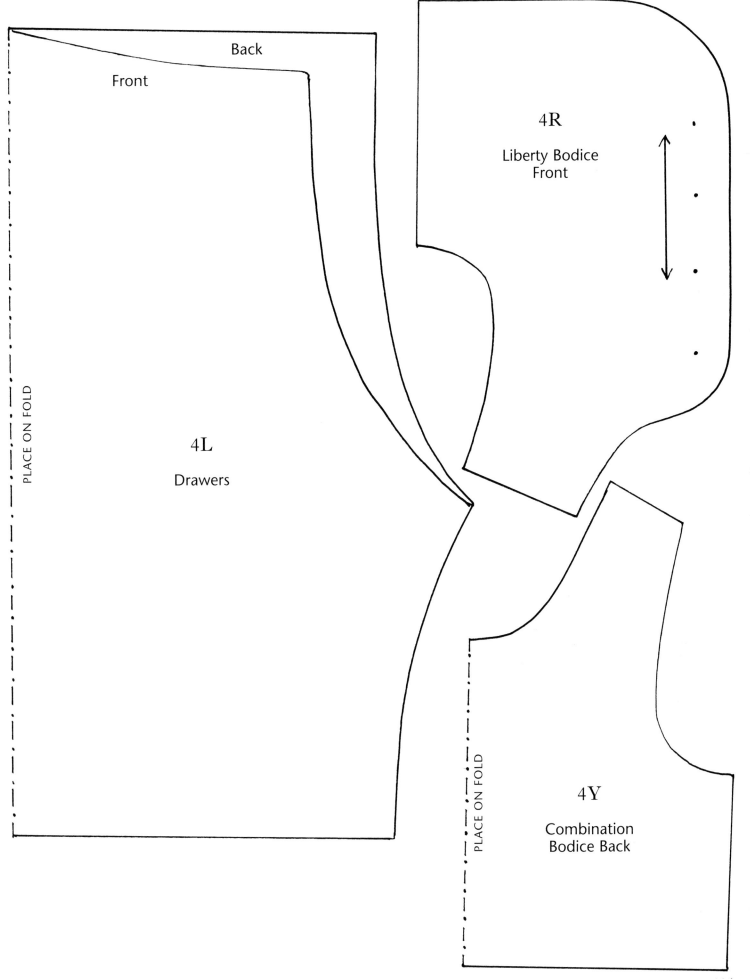

Back

Front

4L

Drawers

4R

Liberty Bodice
Front

4Y

Combination
Bodice Back

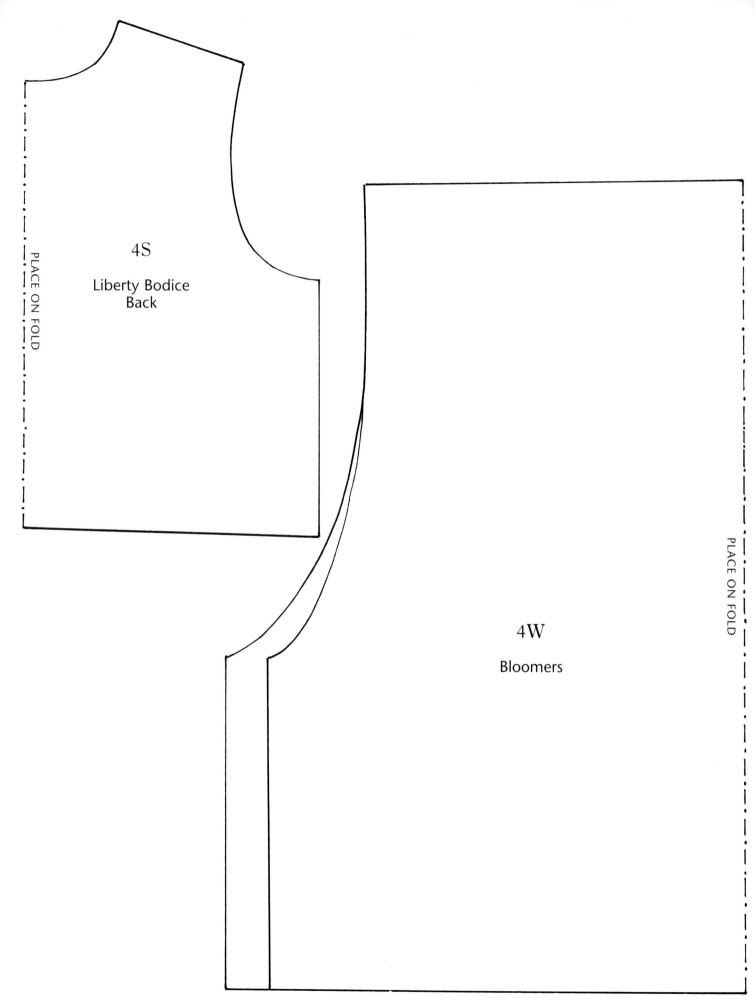

4S

Liberty Bodice
Back

PLACE ON FOLD

4W

Bloomers

PLACE ON FOLD

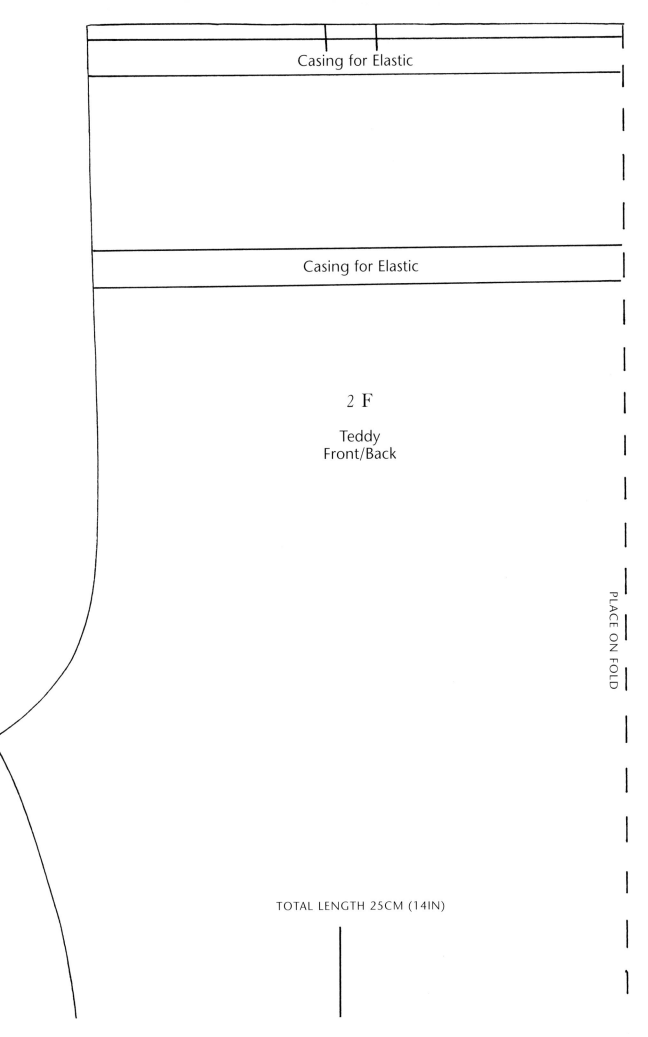

Casing for Elastic

Casing for Elastic

2 F

Teddy
Front/Back

PLACE ON FOLD

TOTAL LENGTH 25CM (14IN)

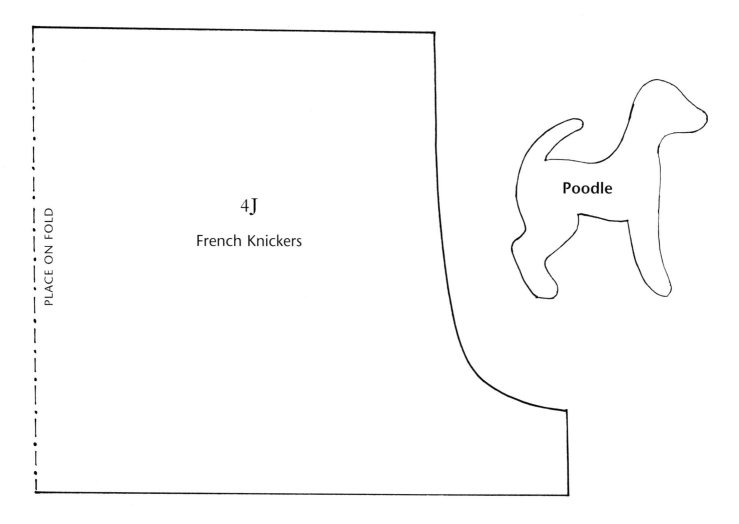

4J

French Knickers

Poodle

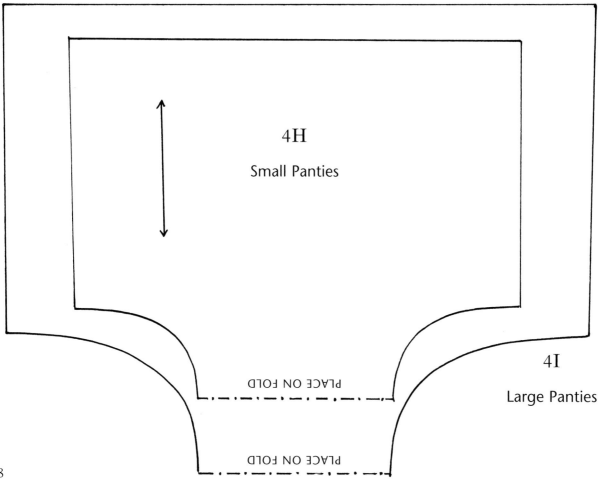

4H

Small Panties

PLACE ON FOLD

PLACE ON FOLD

4I

Large Panties

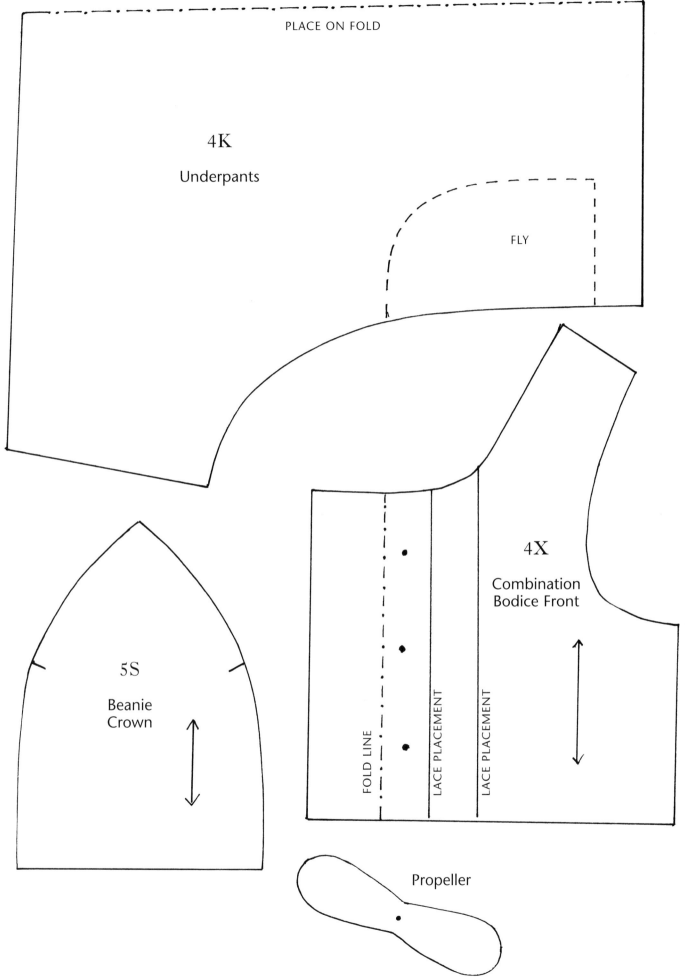

PLACE ON FOLD

4K

Underpants

FLY

5S

Beanie
Crown

4X

Combination
Bodice Front

FOLD LINE

LACE PLACEMENT

LACE PLACEMENT

Propeller

129

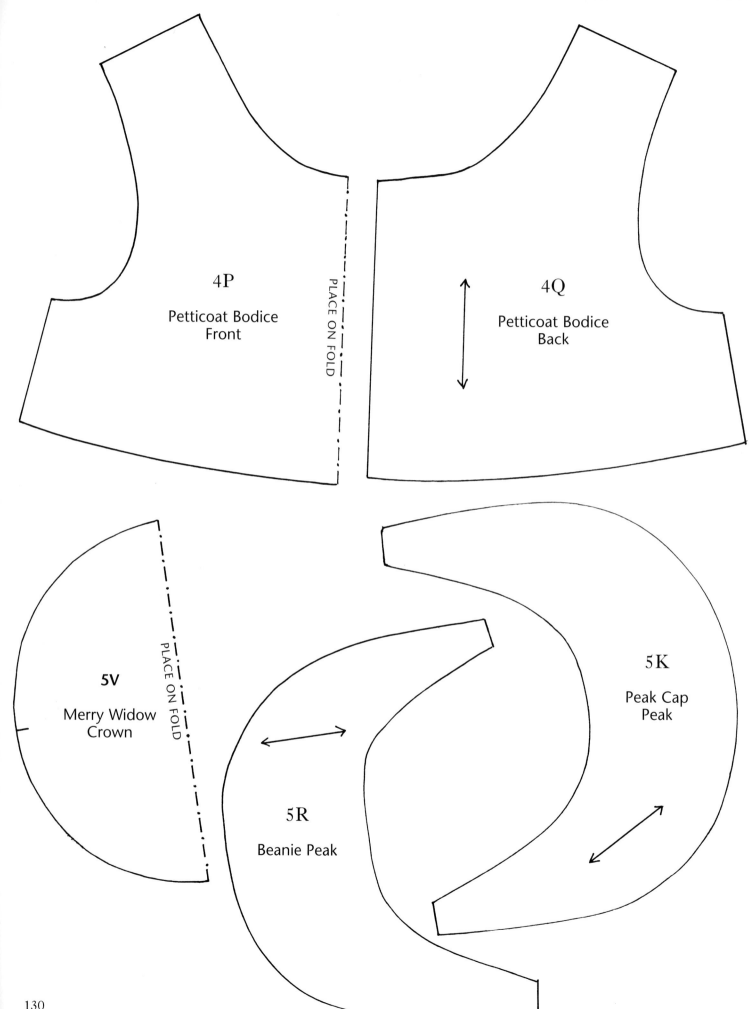

4P

Petticoat Bodice
Front

PLACE ON FOLD

4Q

Petticoat Bodice
Back

5V

Merry Widow
Crown

PLACE ON FOLD

5R

Beanie Peak

5K

Peak Cap
Peak

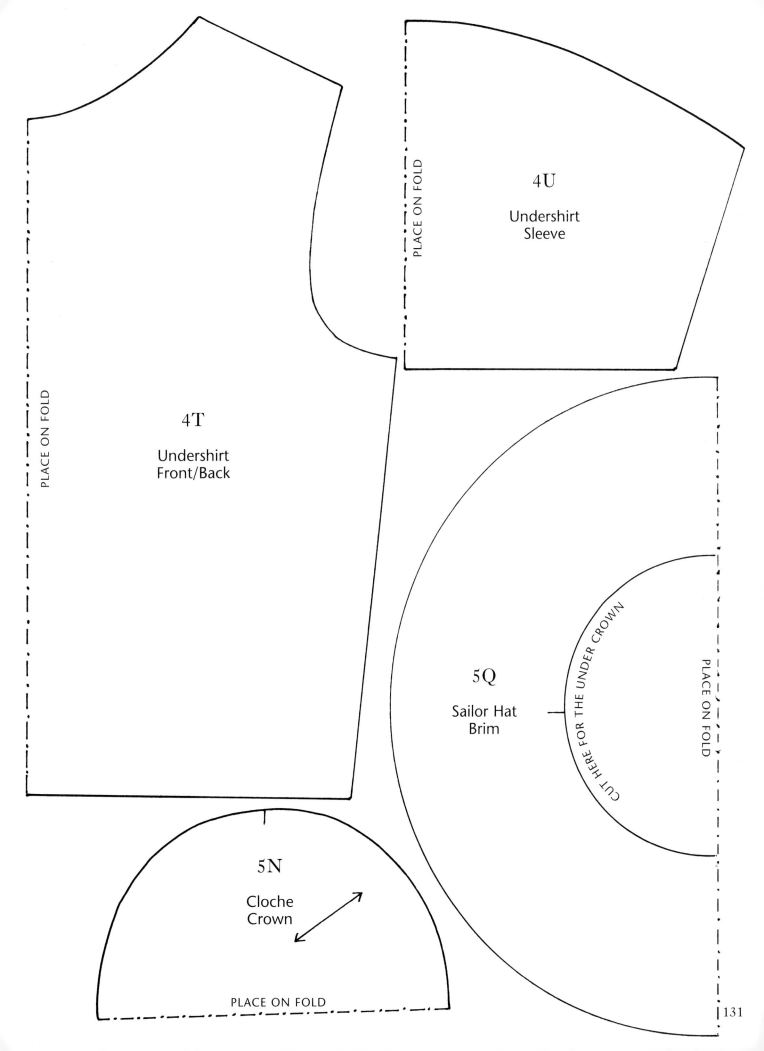

PLACE ON FOLD

4U

Undershirt
Sleeve

PLACE ON FOLD

4T

Undershirt
Front/Back

CUT HERE FOR THE UNDER CROWN

PLACE ON FOLD

5Q

Sailor Hat
Brim

5N

Cloche
Crown

PLACE ON FOLD

131

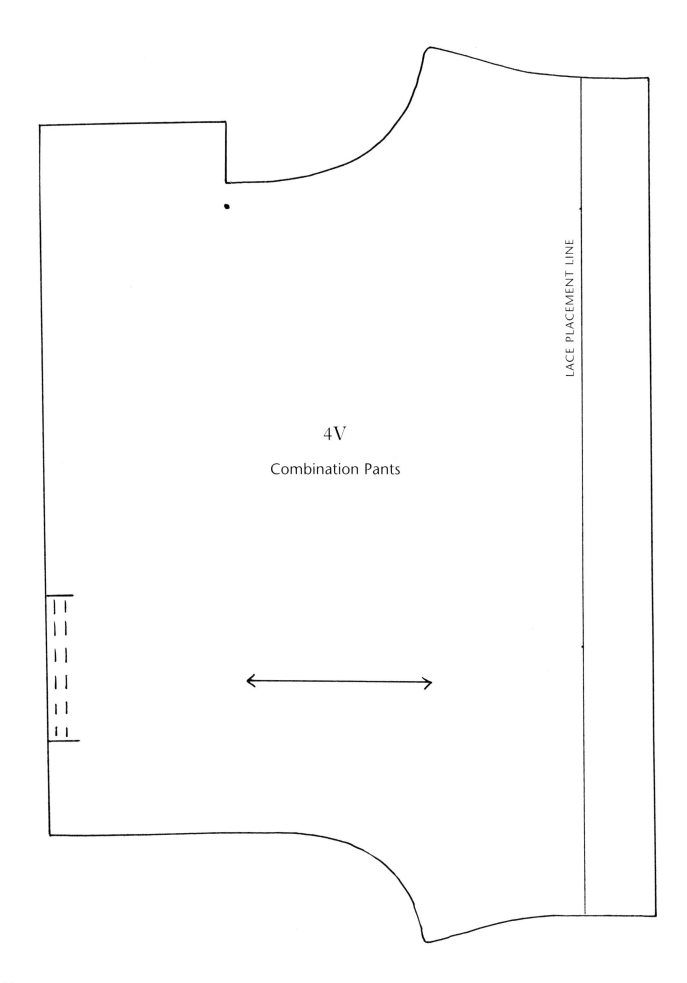

4V

Combination Pants

LACE PLACEMENT LINE

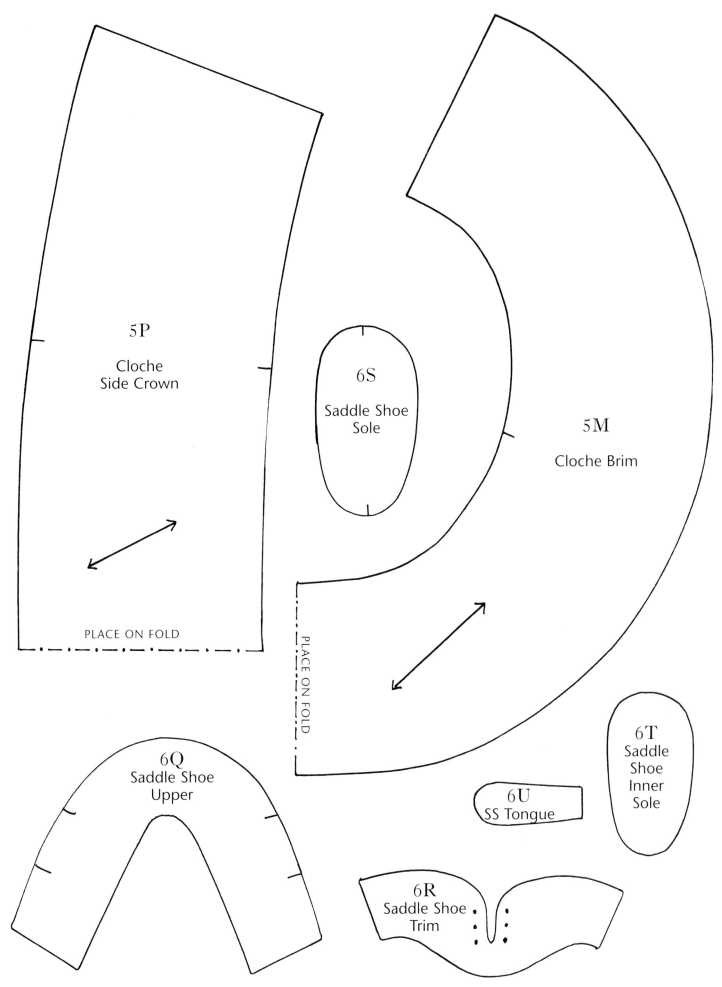

5P

Cloche
Side Crown

6S

Saddle Shoe
Sole

5M

Cloche Brim

PLACE ON FOLD

PLACE ON FOLD

6Q
Saddle Shoe
Upper

6T
Saddle
Shoe
Inner
Sole

6U
SS Tongue

6R
Saddle Shoe
Trim

133

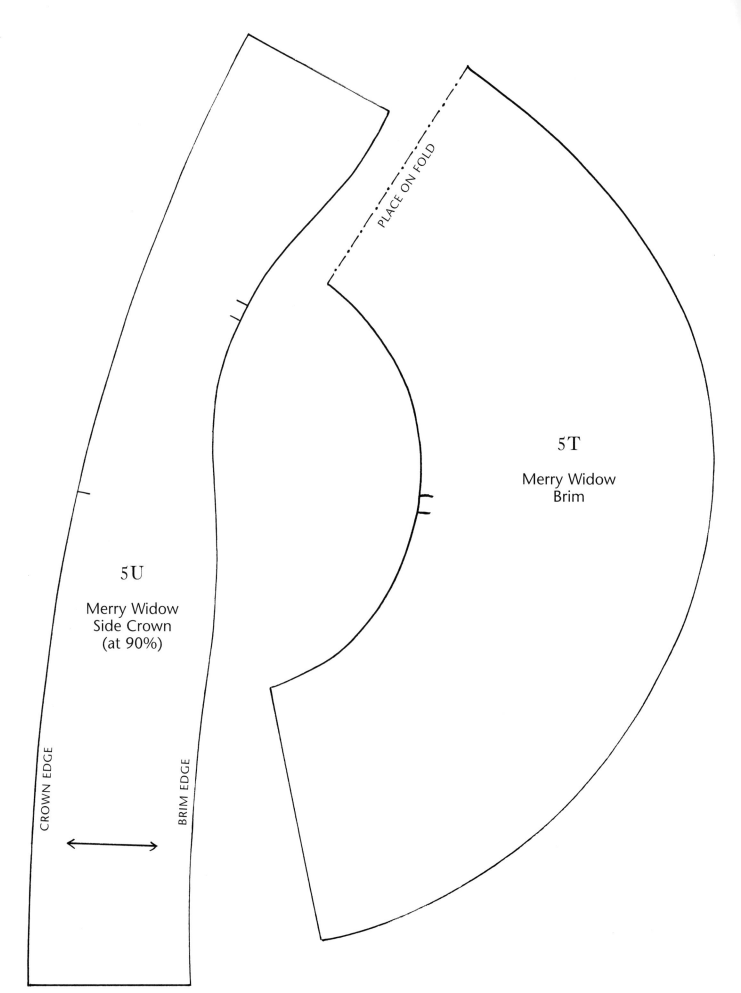

PLACE ON FOLD

5T

Merry Widow
Brim

5U

Merry Widow
Side Crown
(at 90%)

CROWN EDGE

BRIM EDGE

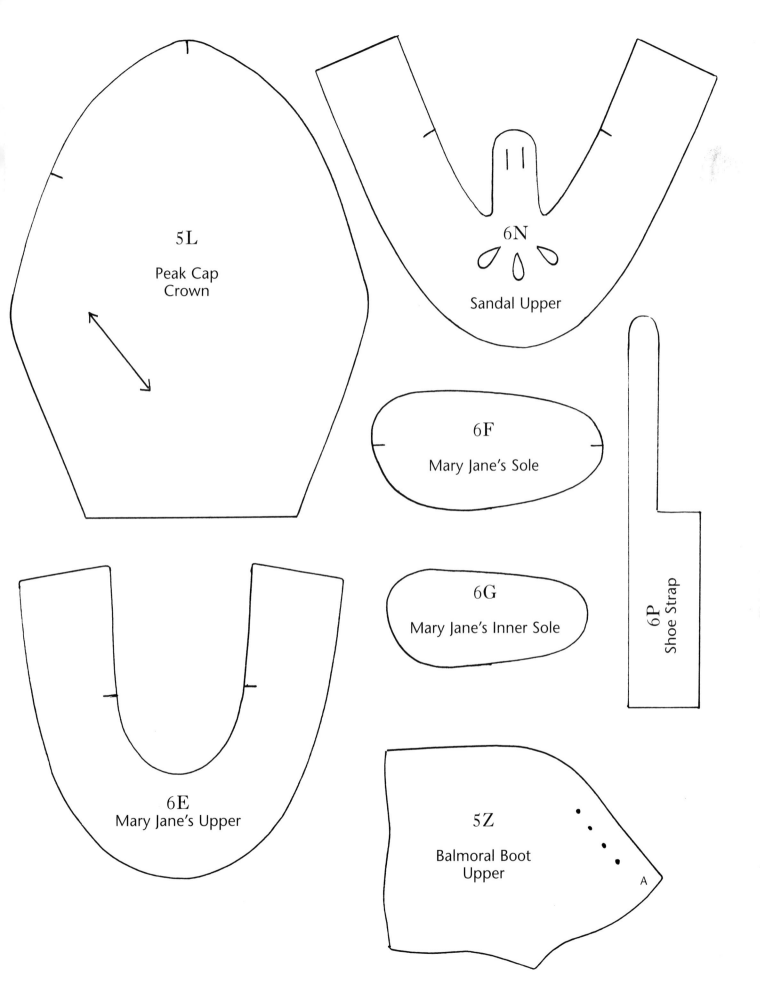

5L

Peak Cap
Crown

6N

Sandal Upper

6F

Mary Jane's Sole

6G

Mary Jane's Inner Sole

6P
Shoe Strap

6E
Mary Jane's Upper

5Z

Balmoral Boot
Upper

A

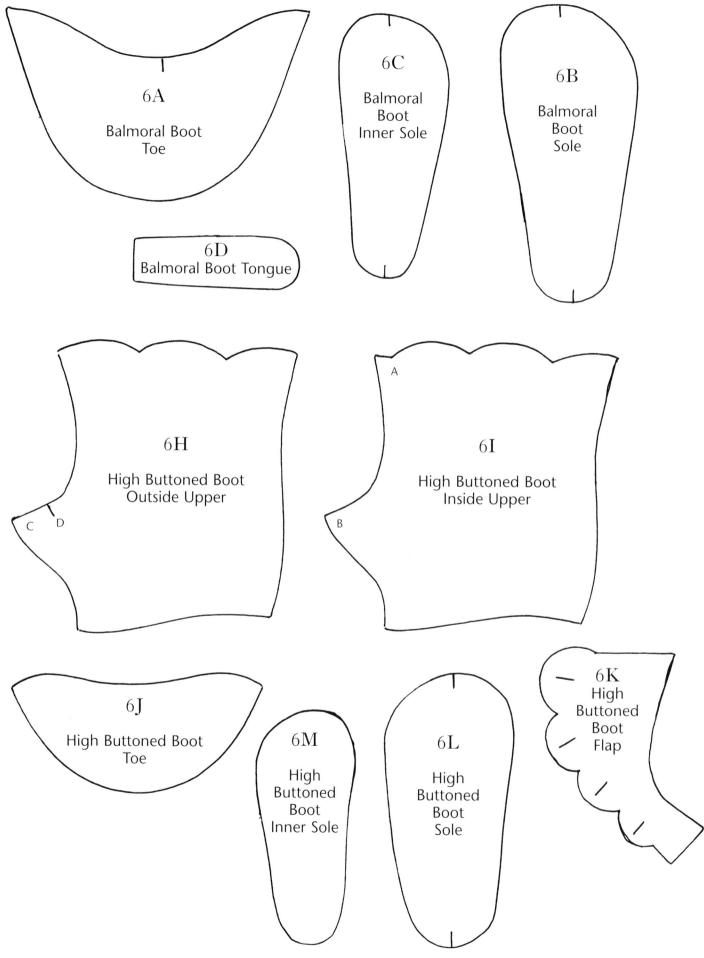

6A

Balmoral Boot
Toe

6C

Balmoral
Boot
Inner Sole

6B

Balmoral
Boot
Sole

6D
Balmoral Boot Tongue

6H

High Buttoned Boot
Outside Upper

C   D

6I

High Buttoned Boot
Inside Upper

A

B

6J

High Buttoned Boot
Toe

6M

High
Buttoned
Boot
Inner Sole

6L

High
Buttoned
Boot
Sole

6K
High
Buttoned
Boot
Flap

Suppliers

Ellie's Doll Workshop
1526 Wimborne Road
Kinson, Bournemouth
Dorset, BH11 9AF
tel: 01202 572626
email:
mike@elliesdolls.freeserve.co.uk
www.elliesdolls.co.uk

Lesley's Dolls
Unit 3, The Depository
Church Street, Warnham
West Sussex, RH12 3QW
tel/fax: 01403 217124
email: sales@expressionsdolls.com
www.lesleydolls.co.uk

Recollect Studios
17 Junction Road
Burgess Hill
West Sussex, RH15 0HG
tel/fax: 01444 871052
email: dollshopuk@aol.com

Acknowledgments

I would like to thank my husband David for his support during the writing of this book and for the lovely little hat stands and clothes rack he took the time to make for my displays

Index